"David's stories touch my heart each week." Susan Ferriby, reader for 20 years

"I have been reading David Smith's essays and reminiscences for many years, first in the newspaper every week and then in his blog. He inspires me to do better as a writer myself, and he makes me think, which is an activity I enjoy a lot." Len Bassham, reader for 20 years

"I always look forward to Monday Moanin'. Sometimes insightful and thought-provoking, sometimes clever and funny, but always entertaining." Richard Skaff, reader for 23 years

"Monday Moanin' is the perfect way to start my week. David's writing is so inspirational." Theresa West, reader for 10 years.

"I get the Monday Moanin' at work and enjoy being transformed to another place thru David's eloquent words. I'm especially grateful to be taken on his runs." Debbie Wheeler, reader for 17 years

"'Monday, Monday. Can't trust that day.' Those were my sentiments until I discovered Monday Moanin'. Now I look forward to starting my week off with David's essays and a cup of coffee." Kay H. Roberts, reader for 12 years

"David's words every Monday Moanin' have made me think, made me smile, and made my day!" Amy Tratt, reader for 20 years

"Monday Moanin' columns are rebellious, as they make what's tangible and ordinary the primary place where extraordinary questions of morality, aesthetics, love, and truth may be answered. (Or, at the very least, wondered about over a cup of coffee.) His writing has inspired me to seek out the true, the good, and beautiful in every moment, not just the big ones. In short, this book is a lovely reminder of all the simple things that matter." Sawyer Smith, reader for 10 years.

"David is a path maker. He lays down words we can use to go places! His style's a little smoother, but David loves life and people like Will Rogers did—and his musings are magical and insightful. Grab this book and a good cup of coffee and prepare to be delighted!" Dallas Gatlin, reader for 9 years

D1452522

Praise from Readers:

"Reading Monday Moanin' is like sitting with a warm cup of tea with a good friend. As David shares his observations about life, we are drawn in by the warmth, humor, and grace in which he weaves his stories that leave us quietly inspired or restored of our faith in this shared human experience." Sunny Beeker, reader for 23 years

"David Smith's Monday Moanin' columns are sneaky. One always reads with the joy of a kid on a carousel smiling as the gentle breeze of David's winsome words flow by. What is sneaky is how he weaves into each paragraph genuine wisdom, heart, encouragement, and profound insight into the human condition, writing with his unique charm, wit, and frequently laugh-out-loud humor." Tom Skaff, reader for 23 years

"I have a short list of favorite authors … writers who show me their own beautifully imperfect humanity even as they challenge me to my best self. David Scott Smith is at the top of that list. Hope This Finds You *is a celebration – a murmuration, if you will – of life, love, wonder, and joy. Those of us who have been reading David's essays for years know full well the treasure we now hold in our hands."* Eileen Button, reader for 15 years

"David writes of situations that are immediately recognizable, but his insights are so simply profound that he turns the ordinary into the extraordinary. Often funny or bringing a tear to the sweet cheek, and sometimes evoking both emotions simultaneously. His essays invite you to look at life's daily gifts, troubles, habits, and emotions in ways that surprisingly transforms your soul." Tom and Jody Wolfe, reader for 23 years

"David's writing touches a place deep within and gives me a sense of grounding. He finds meaning in the simplest experiences of daily life and helps us appreciate and remember what is important." Sabrina Keeley, reader for 3 years

"David's upbeat and optimistic Monday Moanin' column takes the mundane activities in life and may make me laugh or cry. I look forward to starting Mondays with his gentle perspective on daily events, especially his thoughts on being a runner." Sue Weiss, reader for 20 years

"David's humor brings me joy. His insights are profound, and his description of our shared everyday life encounters spot-on. Every Monday starts with his wit and wisdom." Bud Pratt, reader for 23 years

"'Wordsmith' describes David Smith in no uncertain terms. His ability to bring his readers, including me, to tears, laughter, and reflection in his weekly essays is uncanny." Jerry Knoodle, reader for 13 years

"David's gift for writing moves his readers from laughs to tears and back to laughs again within just a few sentences. His thoughtful perspective and captivating storytelling challenge his readers to look at life through numerous lenses, while keeping them engaged and wanting more." Karen Meersman, reader for 23 years

"If you want to immerse yourself in words that pull your mind and emotions into a better place, my friend David makes that possible through his writing. I continue to be grateful for his friendship and thoughtful stewardship of the human experience." Jerry Johnson, reader for 20 years

"Rainy days and Mondays never get me down when I've got David's words to read. I look forward to his words, some simple and some complex, which come together to tell a wonderful story." Ilene Hill, reader for 17 years

"Monday Mornings have been the 'eye of the hurricane' for me. Regardless of how the week is starting, I etch out some time, block out the madness that surrounds me … and I treat myself to David's genius." Douglas Smith, reader for 23 years

"My favorite day of the week is Monday because I start it reading Monday Moanin'. Each week I am taken on a wonderful journey through David's words." Jennifer Sharrer, reader for 23 years

"David is a master storyteller, and I always wait for the lesson to learn. He teaches us to be more observant, to be better people, and to seek and find more fulfillment in life." Linda Tomandl, reader for 15 years

"David's words inevitably bring me pause followed by an immense inner smile with appreciation for the most ordinary happenings all around me." Sally Kelly, reader for 17 years

HOPE

THIS

FINDS

YOU

LETTERS FROM A FRIEND

DAVID SCOTT SMITH

STARLINGS PRESS

HOPE THIS FINDS YOU Copyright © 2022
by David Scott Smith.

For information contact: www.davidscottsmith.net

Cover design by Danna Mathias Steele

ISBN: 979-8-9867341-0-1 (paperback)

ISBN : 979-8-9867341-1-8   (ebook)

First Edition: December 2022

To the readers who join me every
Monday morning

Contents

Preface

March 2016

Greetings from the first scene,

FADE IN:

INTERIOR. DARK BEDROOM.

Close-up of digital clock on the nightstand shows 4:30. Light from window (snowy exterior) casts pale gray on sleeping figure.

Blankets are thrown back and legs appear on the edge of the bed. MAN sits up, runs his hands over his face and fumbles for glasses on nightstand.

(SOUND OF KNEES POPPING AS MAN STANDS UP.)

CUT TO KITCHEN.

MAN stands at the counter pouring coffee beans into grinder. He is wearing tattered flannel pajama pants and a wrinkled t-shirt.

GRINDER: (loud, sarcastically) I bet you wish you had bought grounds instead of beans. Or at least ground the beans in advance. Am I right? Well?

MAN: Could you be a little quieter, please? It's still practically night.

GRINDER: Sure, shoot the messenger. You know this is what I sound like, I'm like this every morning, so now you want to blame me? You're the one who wants coffee.

MAN says nothing and scoops the coffee into the filter. Pours water into COFFEE POT.

COFFEE POT: (whispering) Morning. You look tired

MAN: You say the same thing every morning. Are you showing concern or trying to make me feel old?

COFFEE POT: (sighing softly) Why don't you go wash out your mug while I finish here? Otherwise, you'll get annoyed waiting the two minutes it takes for me to make the coffee.

MAN removes mug from sink and runs hot water, scrubs the mug and dries it and sets it on the counter next to the coffee pot. On the side of the mug is printed three words: "Life is Good."

COFFEE POT: Coffee is done. If I do say so myself, it smells fabulous.

REFRIGERATOR: Just want to remind you that I am fifteen years old. Not sure how much longer I'll last. By the way, you're out of butter.

MAN: (reaching into REFRIGERATOR for cream) Why do you bring this up? I know you are old, really, do we have to discuss this now? I'm not awake yet.

WALL OVEN: You think he's got problems; I am on my last leg here. And I am really expensive.

FURNACE: (OFFSCREEN) Remember how much money I cost?

COFFEE POT: Don't pay any attention to them. Just pour your coffee.

COLLEGE TUITION: (OFFSCREEN) I know I have been talking to you all night about this, but I hope you have made plans for next semester. Last time we talked, you seemed clueless.

MAN pours coffee into mug, stirs in a few drops of cream.

REFRIGERATOR: I don't know why I bother to keep cream at all, you hardly use enough to matter. Every day I work so hard to keep things cool and no one appreciates it. I am really ready to give up.

MAN glances at refrigerator but does not respond. He lifts the coffee to his lips and takes the first taste. He breathes in the aroma and smiles.

(SOUND OF ANGELS SINGING)

CUT TO: DEN

Small desk set against window-lined walls. A single lamp lights the room from the desk. A laptop and some papers sit in the yellow circle of light. It is dark outside, so the reflection of the lamp is on the windows.

MAN walks in holding coffee, sits down at the desk.

(SOUND OF KNEES POPPING AS MAN SITS DOWN)

LAPTOP: I thought you were going to write last night. You never learn. I mean, no pressure, but you don't have a lot of time. What were you doing? Watching the debate?

MAN: (sighing) Really? I just sat down. Can you give me a minute?

LAPTOP: I'm not sure if you heard me last night while you were trying to sleep, but I had all of these really great ideas.

MAN: I heard you. But (sipping coffee) I don't exactly remember what we talked about.

RUNNING WATCH: (FROM DESK) Are you going running this morning? You didn't get a lot of miles in last week.

KNEES: Get off his back. He's not getting any younger

RUNNING WATCH: Look, I don't care how old he is. He committed to me for a certain number of miles and I'm not seeing it. But if he doesn't think it's worth it…

LAPTOP: No pressure here, but if you are going to write anything this morning you better get started.

MAN: Can I at least finish my cup of coffee? I mean, seriously, you have been pestering me all night and I just need a minute to wake up.

COFFEE POT: (OFFSCREEN) Just ignore them. If you want another cup, I'll keep it warm for you. Really, you should think about getting to bed earlier.

LAPTOP: I can't believe you don't remember what we talked about last night. Remember that great idea that you thought was hilarious? Pulitzer Prize and all that?

MAN sets coffee mug on desk and rests hands on the laptop. He licks his lips.

LAPTOP: All right, here we go.

EXTERIOR: View through window of den: MAN sitting at desk, motionless. (SOUND OF SINGLE BIRD CHIRPING. SOUND OF WATER DRIPPING OFF EAVES)

INTERIOR: DEN. MAN sits with hands on laptop. Screen is blank. He is staring at the keyboard.

LAPTOP: Don't you ordinarily press the keys to make words on the screen? Isn't that how the writing activity goes?

MAN: (through gritted teeth) I'm thinking.

STOMACH: Hungry. And a little annoyed.

MAX (small white dog) walks into den and looks expectantly at MAN.

LAPTOP: Come on, we have a lot to do. This can't be that hard. Just start.

MAX: I have to go out. I don't care what you are doing. Stop it now.

STOMACH: If you're getting up to let him out, could you get a banana?

MAN: (to LAPTOP) I have to take care of this.

LAPTOP: (exasperated) Fine! I thought this was important, but go ahead. No pressure.

MAX: Why are you still sitting? Let me out or I will pee on this rug.

RUG: Please let him out.

KNEES: If you are going to keep running you have to stretch more. You could do it now.

(MAN stands up and exits with MAX. Den is empty and quiet except for FURNACE whispering something about utility costs and changing the filter)

MAN returns and sits down again.

MAN: Ok, where were we? (Rests hands on keyboard)

STOMACH: Not getting the banana, evidently. (GRUMBLING) Might want to rethink coffee.

COFFEE POT: (OFFSCREEN) Leave him alone. It's one of his few pleasures.

LAPTOP: It's not that hard. Just push any key to get started. You can do it.

MAX: (OFFSCREEN) I want to come back in right now. Stop what you are doing.

MAN: (to LAPTOP) Come on. Give me a clue. What was it I said that was so funny?

MAX: (OFFSCREEN) I am going to wake the neighbors now and see if they will come let me in. And there are deer out here. And I want to come in.

RUNNING WATCH: (FROM DESK) Wow, look at the time. If you're going to fit in a run, you better get moving.

PILE OF MAIL ON DESK: Looks like your cellphone bill is due. And your car is being recalled. And you should read this magazine you ordered about writing. It's been here for a month. Maybe if you're not interested in writing you should cancel your subscription.

LAPTOP: He is interested in writing. He just needs to get started. Press a key!

MAN: Maybe another cup of coffee will help.

LAPTOP: NO!

STOMACH: NO!

COFFEE POT: (OFFSCREEN) Great idea. You deserve it.

MAN STANDS AND EXITS DEN (SOUNDS OF KNEES POPPING)

CLOSE-UP OF LAPTOP — SCREEN SAVER COMES ON

RUNNING WATCH: (FROM DESK) Is he coming back?

(FADE TO BLACK)

Hope this finds you directing,

David

Hope this finds you growing

*"It may be that when we no longer know
what to do, we have come to our real work
and when we no longer know which way to go,
we have begun our real journey.
The mind that is not baffled is not employed.
The impeded stream is the one that sings."*

~ Wendell Berry

NEVER UNDERESTIMATE THE DAY

May 2019

Greetings from where we prepare,

Over twenty years ago, I started sharing essays with the world in a column I call Monday Moanin'. The start of the week is often filled with a certain anxiety that maybe even soaks into Sunday night. The challenges and responsibilities of the day loom large, and sometimes we have a hard time looking directly at them. On this morning, and every one since I began, I have sought to find a better way to start our week other than dreading it.

Four weeks ago, to the minute, I stood in a hotel room and looked out the window at the wind and rain punishing the city. Trees pleaded for mercy, bent over sidewalks, shredded by the wind, and the few people on the sidewalk were soaked by the monsoon. I watched with a cold lump in my chest, knowing I would be running in that weather, struggled not to let that image ruin my hope. Not many hours later I would line up to run the Boston Marathon. Not a drop of rain fell on me until the last mile, and then it was a welcome, refreshing shower.

Never underestimate the day.

It's human nature to see what could be challenges ahead and try to plan for them. It's a mature reaction to expect that problems will arise and to brace yourself for them, to some degree. If we don't factor in for rain, bring the umbrella, we get soaked. Ah, but life is not just umbrellas. It is what we experience, and what we make of that experience. The quality of our life is not determined by what the weather does, or what people say, or the chaos that sometimes awaits. The full potential of our lives comes from how we fill the moments in anticipation and respond to what comes to us.

I finished my coffee hours ago, already thinking of a list of things that waits for me. Some are less than pleasant. What also crossed my mind is a host of possible problems hovering around in the days to come. I'm betting many of you have already gone through this exercise. We don't have to give in to this. Never underestimate the day.

Some weeks ago, I spoke to a group of training leaders for the *Crim*, a festival of running races in Flint, my home city. I was looking forward to it, felt like I was prepared and that the message was one they would find value in. That morning, I saw the impact of my words was bigger than expected. A few weeks later, I was still running into people who were touched by the words. I had underestimated the day. And me. And them.

Yesterday I ran in the cool morning, feeling the potential in me, feeling it in the gray morning. It reminded me of many other days that started this way, immersed in nature, feeling my body work, and having the time to let my thoughts gather in their own way.

A few miles into the run, I turned up a trail, scattering rabbits and a band of deer, and climbed up a small bluff that overlooked the river there. I stood in the slanted morning light and felt my breath, the pounding of my heart, and the stillness of the forest. A few birds seasoned the moment, and then two woodpeckers added their percussion. The beauty caught me by surprise, filled my eyes with tears.

I left home knowing, expecting an awesome morning, and even so, even feeling the potential, it took me being there to realize I had underestimated what the day held for me.

What I know from just the slightest reflection, the bit of perspective from a few days of experience, is that we will see the beauty and richness of every day if we expect to see it. We will know the kindness and generosity of people if we expect to see it. We will understand that even in rain or wind, even in the exchange with a stranger, or the unknown of the next moment, there is the potential for great things. This color and flavor and power and love wait for us every day, and we only risk missing it if we underestimate the possibilities.

Prepare for the best. There are a few of you who will look askance at this, rolling your eyes at the naïve notion that what we expect has anything to do with reality, with what is given to us. Yes, life happens to us in ways we can't control. It's still our choice where we put ourselves on the spectrum. We don't have to live in fear, we don't have to simply accept that the worst is coming.

The truth is, we are going to have problems today, and tomorrow. What we do with them is up to us, and that will be how we measure the day. Think about that as you process each challenge. Expect that you will handle it the best you can, expect a good outcome, expect that others will be good humans. You can see a rainstorm on the horizon and not agonize over it. Otherwise, you get wet twice.

I'll admit my selfishness here; I'm writing this all for me, really. I must arm myself with these reminders or I will fall prey to the same angst that waited for me yesterday and last week and twenty years ago. What I really want for myself, and for you, is to experience all that waits for me today, rain or shine, with the same spirit of high expectation that has always left me most satisfied in my life. I know I am going to be closest to my best self if I never underestimate the day.

Hope this finds you leaning into the possible,

David

SUMMERSMITH

August 2018

Greetings from the magic,

With each step I run, I pour my magic into the air. Each footfall creates a vibration that changes the world. God leans closer to see what it is and smiles summer on us.

I am in my natural state.

The calendar makes idle threats, but I am not intimidated. I have the power older than dates on paper. I am Summersmith.

How else will summer be? How else will the water know that it should foam and splash at the sandy edges of the world? If I am not out to create the space where the heat can fill, if I don't swirl a cloud of starlings into the sky, if I am not out running to send the message to the cicadas and the crickets, how else will we hold this magic still in the middle of ice and darkness?

Summer cannot just happen; it is not simply astronomy. It is created each morning as I sip coffee on my deck and then grows stronger as I run the two-lane roads. I pass by your windows as you are waking up, and you hear mourning doves, you feel the soft breeze, smell the day, and you know I am at work.

It happens because seeing a cluster of deer walk through my yard still makes me feel like something wonderful has just happened, like I am eight years old and this was created just to amaze me. I know that when I feel this, it pulls summer to us.

I run between the beans and the fences and the yards, and the greenness flows out from me. I run and run and run, and flowers too beautiful to name burst from the ground. Clusters of finches, yellow commas against the shrubs, leap ahead of me to enjoy the warmth I create.

You stood on your porch and listened to the rain on the roof, chuckling into the eaves, and you were carried to when you were a child at your gramma's, or when you were camping, or when you had your first kiss, and it smelled like this day. Because somewhere out there, on shiny-wet strips of macadam, I am running, splashing the magic, making a summer storm.

I run and run and run and heat lightning flashes and the sound of a train floats into your dream undaunted by the screen in your window. I run and the butterfly settles on the leaf, and the sun turns shadows between branches into mysterious daguerreotypes in the dirt.

I run, and the day lasts longer because it wants to; it hates to end. And the sun steps up its game at the western end of the world, promising to do it over tomorrow.

I can't do it alone; there are others too. The little boy on his bike who is creating the world a block at a time, the four girls running through the sprinkler, laughing in their bright bathing suits, turning the yard into eternal June and July. The old man who makes the smell of freshly cut grass. The couple who are grilling chicken, playing *Moondance* on the stereo. Somewhere someone licks the drop of ice cream escaping from the cone onto the back of their hand. Someone tracks sand into the house.

I run to soak in the summer and radiate to the world, so you drive with your top down and the music up. And the Frisbee floats to an impossible catch and the grass feels like silk against your neck as you stare up at the clouds, and the water tastes like the garden hose, and it is the best.

I run and run and run and run, and it is summer and it is summer and it is summer and it is always, forever summer.

This morning I am cupping it all in my hands, my skin the color of August, and I look into the pool of summer there and see my face reflected in it and know. I am Summersmith.

Hope this finds you with the windows open,

David

ANNIVERSARY

August 2020

Greetings from the rooms we share,

In most of life's endeavors, thirty-five years would bring you a certain level of mastery. I submit that marriage is not one of those. Marriage is not plumbing or carpentry or the care of a bonsai. There are myriad reasons we do not master this union, most of which exist in the people joined in it. That is the joy and ache of the thing, and therein is the hope in it.

Thirty-five years ago, on this very date, I walked back down the aisle of a church a different person than I had been when I entered. I was married to Suzanne, and in those first steps, we became witnesses to each other's lives, necessary, as it turns out, as both of us became new people again and again.

In the years that have been filled between that day and this, we have evolved and grown, so much so that strangers would not always recognize us from one place to the next. We were newlyweds, with that dewy aura, and then we turned our eyes to building a life, and we each became a little different, partners in a new way.

And then Katherine was born, and we changed again, and for a moment I couldn't imagine us ever-changing from that exciting life. And then we had triplet sons, Harrison, Carson, and Sawyer, and life was different again, and so were we. Time passed, with all the rigors of raising children to become young adults who could be launched into the world, and those experiences made new people out of Suzanne and me.

I mean no disrespect to my marriage in saying that I have not yet figured it out; in fact, the opposite is true. The fact that it still requires learning and devotion to its success is what has contributed to our longevity and the richness of our lives. Neither of us can take our role as witnesses for granted, because life is dynamic, and we are changing, and the change is demanding.

I am not writing any of this as sage advice. I am still an acolyte, but I am a willing learner. My level of maturity over these last decades has not kept pace with the information on my driver's license, but I am evolved enough to be self-aware. It is not easy being married to me, I'm confident of this. I could illustrate my long list of spousal deficiencies, my reckoning, not my wife's, but by the time you read this, they will have changed and been added to, so the allusion will suffice.

The French writer Andre Maurois said, "A successful marriage is an edifice that must be rebuilt every day." I have considered this and found it true in that the effort must be invested, but to me the edifice is not always being rebuilt as much as added to.

We have been building a house together. In each new part of our lives, we add rooms for ourselves and for the people who have joined us. Here is the first room where we learned who the other was and how we would love. Here is where our new friends came, now knowing us as a couple. Here is where we made plans for other rooms. Here is the room where our first child came to us. Another where we lost children. Another where the boys joined us.

We build these rooms and add on to the life that is coming to us, and in each room we are a little different. Not strangers, just new. But the beauty in this is that we still have all those other rooms, and we can go back and visit and see who we were and how life was. And in all of that, entering each room, we fall in love over and over again with those versions of us and who we are today. We are witnesses to each other to remind both of us of the rooms to look in.

Suzanne and I also build rooms for ourselves. On the day we were married, my friend Tom read a letter to us and the other witnesses there. I keep it in my desk and look at it from time to time, and it is here with me now. Among other things, he urged us to talk and listen, and to give each other room to think our own thoughts. Sometimes my room is a long stretch of road, and sometimes hers is a beautiful yard. Sometimes it is this room where I write, and hers is right there where she reads and creates and sees the future.

It is not lost on me that this house of many rooms is not unlike the place where our Creator waits. As we have been building each room in our lives, we have felt that presence. God is in each room, patiently showing us, explaining in small ways and large the complexities of our life. We are reintroduced to each other by God, these new witnesses in new rooms, giving us the chance to nurture the promises we made thirty-five years ago.

Now we are in a new doorway, a room that holds other futures, other people, other experiences. There are hallways that extend beyond what we can see or may ever see. Our children and grandchildren are in these places. You, whatever version of you that comes, will be welcome there too. Another lesson from Tom, in that warm church thirty-five years ago, was to make room for those in our lives who love us and bring us gifts we would otherwise miss.

Our life as witnesses to each other continues. We love each other and lead each other into the new rooms holding hands, looking into the corners, making choices together about how the space will be as we become new people again, still bride and groom, newlyweds, new parents, and all the rest, and all of the time each other's.

Hope this finds you opening doors to see,

David

A ROOM OF THEIR OWN

September 2003

Greetings from my own room,

Our little family is steadily evolving and growing. Over the years, I have marked the various rites of passage and shared some with you. There are milestones, and there are milestones. Like Katherine's first step. And the first time we didn't have to remind Sawyer to say "excuse me" when he roared out a belch at the dinner table.

This week held a milestone of some significance; we moved the boys into their own bedrooms. This was a big deal, since they have been sleeping in the same room together for over nine years, some of that time in the same bed.

Aside from the sentimental implications, this was also a major step in practical terms. Moving the boys into their own space meant cleaning and painting their room, organizing and dividing their toys, and somehow making three bedrooms out of two.

As I prepared to paint, I had to marvel at their industriousness in leaving their mark on the old bedroom. There were footprints on the ceiling, an homage to Spiderman. There were thousands of holes in the walls, where important papers had been tacked, or targets hung, or socks stapled. After moving a shelf, I discovered ancient hieroglyphics, in crayon and pencil, the origin of which I could not ascertain, even with offers of amnesty.

The boys could not wait to make the move. Sawyer pestered me again and again about when the beds would be put together. Carson kept asking when the room would be painted and went on about where he would put his things. Harrison seemed ambivalent, but underneath simmered an excitement, the anticipation of independence.

But when the moment came to say goodnight, each moving into their own corner of the world, there was some hesitation. Carson told Suzanne, through his tears, that he would miss talking with his brothers as they fell asleep. Harrison, stoic that he is, allowed that he would miss his old room. Later in the evening, Suzanne found him sneaking down the hall for a late-night conference with his brothers.

Last night as I said goodnight to them, each in their own bed, nested among their own things, I had a glimpse of three young men at college, or in their first apartment, and it rocked me a little. I was reminded that I need to delight in this day, and tomorrow, while my children are children.

This morning I thought about Alexander, the brother who waits for us with God. He shared space with Carson, Harrison, and Sawyer for only eight months or so, but I can imagine if life had unfolded differently, he would be as excited about moving into a new room as his brothers are.

About three years ago, I had a conversation with Sawyer that I think of from time to time, and since it's on my mind this morning,

I will share it with you.

The two of us were working in the front yard, raking up grass and old leaves on a warm summer afternoon. Sawyer was talking in his way, a sort of stream-of-consciousness thing, and as I worked, I was only half listening. Until this moment.

"You know Trapper died," Sawyer says.

"No, he didn't," I reply, a little distracted.

"Yes, he did."

"Who is Trapper?" I ask, now paying attention.

"He is Leah's other dog . . . he died. They were all sad, real sad, even they had tears."

"That is sad that the dog died."

"But now he can play with him."

"Who?"

"Alexander, up in heaven."

I stop raking. I am watching Sawyer, who is picking up grass and putting it in piles.

"Oh, right, because Trapper is in heaven," I say.

"Right. So he gets a dog. He is the luckiest."

I wait, but he doesn't say any more, and so I go back to my raking. A little while passes and Sawyer starts talking again.

"You know he looks like Colin."

"Who?" I ask, once again not fully engaged.

"Alexander."

"How do you know?"

"I just remember, because I saw him."

"When?"

"When I was like three years old."

"No, Sawyer, he was already in Heaven when you were three."

Sawyer is throwing whirlybirds in the air, watching them float to the ground.

"But I just remember him anyway," he says.

A moment passes and I continue pulling the rake, urging the grass and leaves into small piles. And Sawyer begins again. "I hope he isn't getting into trouble."

I say nothing, waiting to see what he is talking about.

"I hope God is taking care of him."

"Who? Trapper?"

"No, Alexander. Is Alexander still a baby or will he grow up just like us?"

I swallow hard. I am looking down at the grass, but my vision is blurred, and all I see is a green and yellow mosaic.

"I don't know Sawyer. That will be the first thing I will ask God when we see him."

"But how will we remember?"

"Remember?"

"Remember to ask God about it."

"I will write it down."

"Ok Dad, but not right now. Write it down later."

I did write it down later. Word for word.

My children are skimming through their childhood, taking their bruises and cuts, basking in sun, and rolling in the snow. They are learning to ride bikes, learning to play piano, learning to multiply fractions, learning what friends are. Every hurdle and challenge leads to growth; every milestone is a marker of their journey into a full, satisfying life. Every day that passes moves them closer to the day when they will be on their own, filling rooms of their own, with families of their own.

To someone looking in, it would appear there are four children on this journey, but we still see them as five, counting Alexander, who waits for us in the house with many rooms. I hope that he has his own room if he wants and can play with Trapper. He is the luckiest.

Hope this finds you with someone to talk to as you fall asleep,

David

GROWING UP TOO FAST

November 2004

Greetings from beneath the beauty,

I was putting away dirty dishes and pushing the disorder of the kitchen into some form of ordered chaos when Harrison came up to me.

"Dad, can I have a hard-boiled egg?" he asked. When I hesitated, he said, "I'll do it myself, I know how to make them."

I was a little taken aback. Not so much at what he said but the confidence in his voice. I thought perhaps somehow he had paid attention to Suzanne making hard-boiled eggs and absorbed the process. Or maybe she had been teaching him things in the kitchen when I wasn't around. Either way, he was determined he was going to have hard-boiled eggs, and he didn't need me to get them. My son was growing up.

I told him he could make his eggs and then I sat down to watch. I had a feeling that this was something significant, something I would remember. A turning point, when my ten-year-old son begins walking toward independence.

While Harrison was rummaging around looking for just the right pot, I began thinking about something my daughter had said a couple of days before. I had just walked in the door from work and she rushed me, blurting out that next year she could take driver's education. She asked if she could drive to Ludington next summer.

I'll admit I was a little distracted at the moment, still a little rattled from work and driving and tripping over the accumulation of wealth in the garage. I didn't really absorb what she said or give her an answer. It wasn't until I watched Harrison fill a pot with water for his eggs that what she had said hit home.

Back in the kitchen, Sawyer came in and asked Harrison what he was doing. Harrison explained and Sawyer asked him if he would make him some eggs too. This was becoming more interesting all the time.

When I didn't answer Katherine about driving next year, I'm not sure what she might have thought of my reaction. Honestly, I was still concentrating on the vestiges of my own problems at work. A little while later, she came to me and asked: "Dad, do you think I'm growing up too fast?"

I wasn't ready for that question either. This might be the beginning of a trend for me; the inability to answer seemingly simple questions.

Harrison and Sawyer now had selected the four eggs they wanted. They had filled the pan with water. Sawyer began searching for salt and pepper and got out forks and plates. Where this industriousness coming from? These were the same boys who must be literally dragged from bed each morning and propped in front of their breakfast, which better not be out of their reach.

After giving some thought to Katherine's question, I finally answered. "Yes, I think you are growing up too fast, and there isn't anything anyone can do about it." I explained that this was actually the progression that God planned, and it wasn't bad, but it was too fast for all of us. I told her to enjoy being who she was today and not get too frantic for time to pass. It was as close to a philosophy lesson as I could impart to a fourteen-year-old when I hadn't even had my dinner yet.

Harrison was now ready to complete his masterpiece. He gently placed the eggs into the pot of water. Then as we all watched, he lowered the pot into the sink and stood back.

I waited. Sawyer was watching him, confidence in his brother written all over his face. We all waited.

Evidently, there was one step in the process of making boiled eggs that Harrison had missed: the boiling part. I sat still as long as I could, trying not to laugh, as Harrison and Sawyer waited for the eggs to boil and cool in the pot of water sitting in the sink. Before he could reach in and crack the first egg, I stepped in wearing my best "Dad" face.

This morning, I came down early to my den to write. I have been up since before 4:00, shaken awake by things I can't name now. I puttered around making coffee and clearing a place at my desk, trying to herd my brain in the direction of coherent thought. I took the dog out to do his business and as we stepped into the crisp morning air, I was stopped by what I saw. All the ideas that were in my head a few moments before were wiped clear. I stood there for a few minutes while the dog sniffed for just the right spot, and then hurried him back inside and went to wake Katherine.

Katherine and I stood in the backyard and looked up into the sky, still black in the early hours, stars filling the expanse from horizon to tree line. Painted across this entire stunning array was the Northern Lights, the most brilliant display I have seen in my life.

The lights danced across the sky, licking up from the northern horizon halfway to the southern reaches. It looked like the sky was on fire, not a consuming destructive fire, but with a vibrancy, an impossible energy that shone across the heavens.

We stood there in our winter coats and our pajamas and both of us were reduced to children. Time stopped for a few minutes. We stood in awe of this mysterious beauty, our mouths open, lost for words. A shooting star snuck across the sky. The Northern Lights pulsed and ebbed in response.

"It looks like someone is touching the sky with their fingers," Katherine said. I went inside to wipe the tears from my eyes, leaving my daughter to bask in God's gift.

I had told Katherine she was growing up too fast, believed that all my children are growing up too fast, and it wasn't until this morning that I realized that I was too.

Hope this finds you taking your time,

David

FISHING

September 2002

Greetings from the bank,

If you live in the Great Lakes state of Michigan, you likely have been fishing. There are lakes and creeks and rivers of all sizes packed with fish of all sorts. The roads are filled with people dragging their boats, often past one another, to the best fishing spots. You'll find anglers on bridges, in boats, wading in creeks, and on the shores of any body of water large enough to support life. You'll find them fishing in all seasons, including the winter, when all you have to do is cut a hole in the ice to get at the fish.

In more than four decades of Michigan living, I might have been fishing four times. Evidently, I do not have the fishing gene in my DNA. So, I made a little moaning noise when I learned that this week's Cub Scout adventure included a trip to a small pond to go fishing.

We came to our little fishing expedition relying on the kindness of strangers, since we don't own any fishing equipment. Our preparation to fish included putting on bug spray and sharpening sticks to roast marshmallows on. The only way we were going to catch fish was if I could talk them into giving themselves up or lure them ashore with a toasty marshmallow.

The other fathers were men with knives on their belts. Somewhere at home they had nets and waders and hip boots. They have hats with lures stuck in them, and they know where to buy a license in what season. They know where to go to find the fish and how to tempt them out of the water. They know how to cast and how to twitch the rod to make the line jump for the fish. They know how to clean the fish so there is something edible when the job is done. Standing in their company, I was an imposter.

I watched them open their tackle boxes with the little fold-out drawers, filled with sinkers and bobbers, hooks, line, spoons, plugs, Dipsey sinkers, spinners, snubbers, barrels, and all manner of colorful lures. I listened as they talked about rigging: split shot, Texas, wacky, trolling. All I could hope was that no one would ask me about wacky rigging. I'm pretty sure I missed that in driver's education.

Our Scout den took pity on us and loaned us a couple of poles, pointing us toward the pile of tubs containing the worms we would use for bait. Since I am the Dad, I was nominated to handle the slimy work. I followed the example of the seven-year-old kid next to me. Cut the worm in half (using your fingers, you sissy). Impale it on the hook. Try not to shred the worm into tiny pieces while doing this, or it dissolves when it hits the water.

Once you are prepared with your hook baited, however tentatively, you must now cast your line into the water. That's where the fish are. Waiting for the fish to evolve enough to walk out of the water is not very efficient.

In the company of men, one never asks for help; it just isn't done. If I was going to show my sons how to catch a fish, it was going to be using the tried-and-true Smith method: Wing It.

You probably have seen movies of people fly fishing, casting graceful loops of line over the water, placing the hook neatly in the places fish are likely to be waiting. This was nothing like that. It was more like watching someone have a sneezing fit.

I stood at the bank, watching the others cast their lines. I shadowed their moves as best I could; hold the rod back over my head, push the button down on the reel, and fling the rod forward just as you release the button. Perfect.

The first cast goes straight into the mud bank. The second cast loops back around the pole. Then I cast into the weeds. Caught two little yellow flowers. Cast into the grass behind me. Didn't catch anything and the worm escaped. Worms are not smart, but this worm knew I was embarrassing myself and didn't want to be a part of it.

Before long, the boys were flinging their lines into the water with the natural ease of those who aren't trying too hard. Catching fish in this little pond was not a problem. The fish were more than willing to give up a little time in the water in order to provide sport for our boys. No sooner did the line hit the water, there was a fish waving his fin at us to reel him in. I suspect the fish had heard about my prowess as an outdoorsman and were taking pity on me.

The boys caught fish after fish, giving out the appropriate whooping scream at each strike. Some fish were so small that it was a close battle between the worm and the fish.

Once you have the fish, you must take it off the hook so you can throw it back in the water to catch it again. Since my job was to handle the slimy work, I released the fish. After a few, I was actually pretty good at getting the hook out without hurting anyone, other than the minor insult to the fish. I threw a lot of little fish into that pond. I swear one of them looked at me like, "You again?"

We made our way back to our car in the fading light, the boys running ahead with their pals, mighty hunters, hollering boy stuff to each other. They were exuberant, filled with pride over their new accomplishment. We had conquered fish and the fear of failing to fish. Another adventure, another memory that will stay with us, long after I get this smell off my hands.

Hope this finds you getting a nibble,

David

TOWELS

September 2004

Greetings from a guy with dry wit,

Once a week the Laundry Fairy arrives, and I magically get clean clothes and towels. I learned about the Laundry Fairy when I asked Suzanne about where all the clean towels went, and she said, "Why don't you ask the Laundry Fairy?" in a tone that gave me the feeling my wife is really mad at the Laundry Fairy. This leads me to believe the Laundry Fairy might be stealing my towels.

Follow along: Day One I have a linen closet filled with about twenty clean bath towels. I took a shower on Day One and used one towel. Suzanne took a shower using two towels, one for her hair, which I do not begrudge her, although I never have seen the need for such extravagance. By Day Two, all the towels are gone.

I discovered this at a rather inopportune moment, as I stepped from the shower in full towel-anticipation. The feeling of towellessness overwhelmed me.

I launch a full-scale investigation. I scour every inch of the house, looking everywhere a towel could be wadded or folded. I find laundry baskets conveniently located in each child's bedroom. Dirty clothes are conveniently located on the floor surrounding the laundry basket. I hope this does not prevent the Laundry Fairy from making her appointed rounds. No towels.

Most of the towels that are used in the traditional manner are easy to find because they are still lying on the floor in the immediate area of use. Except for the one that is a semi-permanent turban on my daughter's head.

I have one son, Harrison, who is an aspiring superhero, so one towel is a cape. Ironically, last night as he emerged from the shower, he could not find a towel and had to dry himself by rolling on the carpet. The other two sons tell me they have no idea where the towels are. I show them pictures of the towels and they both deny ever having seen a towel in their life. Just for good measure they both also deny knowing where my hammer is.

I seem to remember someone blotting up something the dog left on the kitchen floor, so that accounts for another towel, one which I will not go looking for. That is a total of six towels accounted for.

It goes without saying that in a house like ours, some towels will be used for sarong duty or as a temporary tent for basement bivouacs. (By the way, whenever something goes without saying, you can count on someone saying it.) Anyhow, I expect a certain number of towels have been diverted from their original intent, but after serious investigation I have determined that my towels have been taken by the Laundry Fairy or are hidden in Iraq, where you can hide almost anything.

By Day 3, I am using a beach towel with Scooby-Doo and Shaggy on it. Then after that, the one odd towel with the name of the famous hotel on it that I swear I've never been to and did not take anything from.

Once these are used, I must resort to the thin, frayed, demi-rags we call the Second-String Towels. Second-String towels are unraveling at both ends, one string at one end and a second string at the other. It takes several of these towels to equal the moisture retention of an ordinary Q-tip. They are the towel-equivalent of congressmen; they look good folded up just sitting there, but really can't perform any function.

I've given up looking for linens, thrown in the towel, so to speak. It's possible that the Laundry Fairy has them, or perhaps our maid. Yes, it turns out we have a maid! I asked Suzanne when the mess in the kitchen was going to get cleaned up and she said, "Why don't you ask the maid?"

Hope this finds you with a towel right out of the dryer,

David

IRONING

October 2007

Greetings from Hazel,

Here is a bundle of cloth, wound into a shapeless clot of cotton. You might imagine it as a turban, or a vest, or some kind of large bandage. In fact, at least in its most recent incarnation, it was a pair of khaki pants.

In the long list of futile phrases, starting with "Turn off the light when you leave the room," we add, "Hang those pants up so that they won't get all wrinkled."

All summer our boys have rolled out of bed and into a pair of shorts, often still standing rigid from where they were propped the night before. Add some sandals and a shirt that was close to the top of the laundry basket and the ensemble is complete.

But now they are back in school, and temperature and decorum dictate a slightly more formal couture. Not exactly black tie, but at the minimum the clothes they wear should appear as though they don't normally double as pajamas. Or turbans.

Suzanne does the laundry, an endless duty in our house. One by one the kids have been taught to do their own laundry, and with some success. There is a major blind spot when it comes to folding the clothes, an inherited deficiency from me, I'm afraid. This can sometimes lead to a version of laundry folding best described as "wadding."

The boys' laundry baskets, filled with clean clothes, will stand guard in front of empty drawers, and as the week passes, dirty clothes will pile up on the floor nearby. Each morning they will root through the basket for something clean, and hopefully find it, or else they will be forced to choose from the inventory on the floor.

Add to the list of futile phrases, "Take your clean clothes to your room and put them in your drawers." The last half of that sentence might just as well be, "… and turn the music up real loud."

Because my sons inherited the wadding gene from me, I feel compelled to compensate for it, and God in his mercy has given me the gift of ironing. This is not exactly biblical, so don't try to find "clothes pressing" in Corinthians.

I don't mind ironing; it's a mindless task, one thing I am eminently suited for. I have a certain knack for it, although not so proficient that a career change is imminent. I can unfold the ironing board with one hand, know how to fill the iron's reservoir with water without getting electrocuted, and have learned after only three episodes not to test with my tongue to see if the iron is hot enough.

I can stand in the laundry room in front of a small window and conquer wrinkles. In the backyard, especially this time of year, deer might wander by, flanked by a constant phalanx of rabbits there. One cannot watch the peaceful scene for too long for fear of scorching a collar or burning an errant finger.

The dryer hums, sometimes with a mild counterpoint provided

by tennis shoes, and makes the room warm. It's not exactly cozy, it's a laundry room after all, but it's nice.

Outside the laundry room door, a boy waits in his underwear. We are minutes from leaving for church and he has been sent to his room twice for a costume change and finally appeared with a good pair of khakis, which have been carefully stored since last spring using the Smith method of scrunch, clump, and roll.

The khakis look like a relief map of Kazakhstan. I remove the few lumps in the pockets, a lint-covered piece of something and a candy wrapper. And a ChapStick. I rev up the iron, little puffs of steam shoot into the air, and subdue the topography in front of me.

There are far better uses of my time. One could easily make the case for professional dry cleaning and clothes that are "wrinkle-free" out of the dryer. The boys can be taught to manage this task on their own. I don't really need to be Iron Man.

I started a list of all the things I can give my children, some of which will never be appreciated or acknowledged, which is the tattoo all parents bear. This thing, this small occasional gift of service, is so easy to do, that I almost hate to give it up. Selfish of me, but I want to hand them a freshly pressed pair of pants, still warm from the iron, and see the look on their face when they put them on. It is not a noble endeavor, but it is one worth doing.

Time enough for them to figure out how to do it on their own, or how to eliminate the need. I can give this little thing to them, a tiny accent to the work that Suzanne pours out for them every day, and enjoy the results, which probably last longer than any advice I've given them.

Hope this finds you in permanent press,

David

SYNCHRONICITY

February 2019

Greetings from human nature,

I stood on the edge of the world, looking out into a waterscape that stretched out into the line that met my imagination. I soaked in the quiet; the only sound was what I brought: my breathing. The wind did not reach me here. The waves, usually chuckling at the sandy shore, were silenced. They were frozen in place, white sculptures of what they will be later. Shaped by an artist whose gallery is everywhere.

I felt the thin air teasing frost at my face, felt it reach the damp places on my skin. I stood there until I felt the cold creep into my muscles, already chilled from the run. I looked down the shoreline, saw the bluffs fifteen miles to the south, dramatic sentinels. The world, in that moment, was still and silent, made that way for me by my companion.

Yesterday I ran along the coast of Lake Michigan, even in the middle of it questioning the sensibility. Snow streamed across the road like wraiths, shaped by low wind, snaking toward me and then vanishing around me. Cold. Snowflakes danced near me, in orbit like planets around me, perhaps tiny worlds with whole frozen civilizations watching me as they carrom by.

A murmuration of snow appeared in the dunes next to me, swirling in the wind, funneling up toward the bruised sky, purple and gray marbled with the white wisps of winter. I stood near the frozen edge of the water and soaked in Nature, felt her hands on me. I was so still that I could sense the thud of my heart making the tiniest motion in my body.

I had this time because I earned it. I ran beyond the cold that numbs the muscles until they don't work, Nature's way of telling me I should never take her for granted. I ran until the road ran out, and then until the path ran out, and finally until the earth ran out.

In that quiet-quiet, with no distractions, no thoughts of anything but that moment, I realized again that when I am too far from Nature, when I don't spend enough time immersed in her, I lose a little of myself.

I have run this same road in summer, the season I was born for. I move easier, my body works better in the warmth, and I welcome that, the feel of the sweat on my skin, the sun on my back. I've felt the heat baked in the dunes, heard the wind applauding in the birches, watched the green waving over the sand. I have run through these same woods, across this same beach when Nature was lighter, more colorful, friendlier. I've stood at the water's edge and watched the incessant exchange of the water and earth. It's easy to love Nature when she is so welcoming.

Winter is a different challenge to run in, but more and more I recognize that Nature in the less hospitable seasons is not the enemy. The idea that I could love Nature, what she brings to our lives, and only be a companion in the best of seasons is so narrow-minded I have a hard time writing the words. I have thought of Nature in winter as hostile, dangerous even. If not malicious, then at best indifferent to me.

But that is not even close to the truth. She is simply who she is. She has the world to make possible for everything living, and to think of her as simply something beautiful to look at does not do justice to what she is for me, or for any of us. Like any good relationship, it takes understanding and adapting to make it work. If I leave the house expecting it always to be summer, there is only one of us that suffers. Nature is patient but rarely indulgent.

I have always had a connection with her. We are not simply acquaintances, and every year the relationship grows in its synchronicity. I respect her, I see her beauty and complexities and feel her power. I also know she does not exist simply for me. And that she is at her best when I am at my best.

I have climbed her mountains, explored the paths that led to waterfalls, to hidden glades. I have run along rivers, ridden across her deserts, slept in her lush meadows, the feel of grass holding me. I have had quiet moments to read in the sun and wild, heart-pounding experiences that still make me smile. It is a rare night that she does not reach through my open window and whisper what waits for me in the world.

And there have been many times when Nature challenged me. She has scraped off the comfortable and the easy and showed me what she shows all animals in her domain. She says to me, in the quiet-quiet; If you want to live the fullest life, to know the entire breadth of experience, then know that on some days you will be tested to your limits. And when you pass through that, you will see what you are made of, and made for.

All of my life, when I am paying attention, Nature restores me. If I make the time to surround myself with her, to soak her in, I return to the everyday routines a stronger, more balanced animal. It is a foolish person who ignores this gift, even in the harshest winter.

I left the iced beach and ran south again, the road held in place by Nature. The trees were charcoal sketches against the flannel horizon. Above me, the gray swollen clouds looked like they would pour coal on the world.

The sand dunes were sensual shapes blanketed in snow. The dune grass fringed the mounds of sleeping earth, feathers riffling in the wind. Sand leaked out from under the snow, hibernating but testing the air to see if it was time yet. A jagged line of birds battled the currents above me. The wind picked up and pressed against my chest to say, "You will have to work harder to go home, but the appetite you create will be that much more pleasant to satisfy."

I am made stronger by her, given balance, inspired by her beauty and the myriad intricacies that make her possible. I don't know what I give back in this exchange, but I can only hope that the time I spend in Nature's company helps fulfill whatever destiny she was created for.

Hope this finds you au naturel,

David

THE GARDEN

June 2019

Greetings from where we grow,

He walked into the hardware store, the wooden screen door banging lightly behind him, and followed the creaking pine boards, shiny and yellow with age, back between the dusty shelves. He had been in this store years before and had a sense of where he could ask for help, at a big counter wedged in the rear of the store.

His short-sleeved plaid shirt was buttoned to the collar, and in the pocket a matching pen and mechanical pencil standing ready for duty. His small round glasses sat exactly where he put them and looked as though they were pinching his eyes together in a permanent scowl.

He stepped to the counter and cleared his throat, his way of announcing himself, a feature of irritation to his wife when she was alive, God rest her anyway.

The woman behind the counter looked up over half-rimmed

readers and looked down again. She was sprinkling eightpenny nails into a metal tray, weighing out five pounds. She wore a stained apron over her denim shirt. The apron was pinned with a name tag that said "Roger."

He cleared his throat again and then in his precise speech made an attempt at a salutation in order to introduce what he really wanted to say. "I have a problem in my garden. I am told you are a good person to advise me in this situation."

The woman paused and rested her hands flat on the counter, strong hands, blunt fingers, a rim of dirt under the nails, a horseshoe scar on the thumb, pale against her tan skin. "How can I help you?" she said with a faint smile, but not putting a lot into it.

The man adjusted his feet and stood a little taller. "I have planted the garden and whatever good that grows is taken by other creatures. I am left to fight weeds that threaten to take over the rest of the patch." He punctuated this statement by thrusting his chin slightly forward, which his wife, God rest her anyway, told him made him look irritated. This time it did, and he was.

"I spend all my time pulling weeds, and it makes me angry. It is not why I planted the garden."

The woman reached up and removed her glasses. She asked what he planted and when, and what he did to keep the poachers out, and what weeds were growing, and what he did about that. It was an interview more than a conversation, neither offering anything much beyond what was required. The man felt himself growing uncomfortable, but he needed her help.

Finally, she put her glasses back on and turned to the shelves behind her, and after pushing a few things aside, found a paper bag spotted with grease stains. She took it down and looked at the man again.

"You were here before, and I gave you what to plant. You may have not understood, or you ignored what you were given. You planted what you thought was sensible or what you saw other people growing. What came up was small and dull with little flavor, but it was what you planted. You were given seeds that would bring you a rich full harvest and you practically ignored the gift."

The man drew himself up slightly, acted as if he had a response, and then thought better of it.

"It's not too late for the garden. I know how to help you, but before I do, you have to agree to trust me and do exactly as I instruct you." She cocked her head slightly and looked him directly in the eye, and in that moment, where he might have looked away, he was frozen in her gaze. He nodded silently.

She reached into the paper bag with a large scoop and brought out a share of the seeds inside and poured them into a smaller bag that magically appeared in her other hand. She rolled down the top. Then, pulling a pencil from somewhere in the large gray bun of hair on top of her head, she scribbled a note on a yellowed pad, tore off the sheet, and stapled it to the bag.

She looked at him one last time, now a hint of kindness in her eyes. "When you plant, don't wear gloves. You should have your hands in the soil. You should feel the earth and it should feel you."

The season ebbed and pulsed, and the days warmed, and the rain fell, and morning broke. The man stood at the edge of the garden in his dungarees and t-shirt he wore to do chores. His lips were set in a straight line. In his hand was the folded note from the hardware store. He had planted as she instructed and watered and stood watch. Last night when he went to bed, there were a few buds in the dark earth. Now what he saw made his legs tremble.

The plants were gargantuan. They were so large they had consumed the entire garden and were pushing up the grass near the tilled soil. Enormous stalks festooned with broad leaves, each tipped with a glorious flower. And under the leaves, incredibly, were pears. And apples. And cucumbers and tomatoes and broccoli. Vines shot out into the grass, heavy with grapes.

He sat on the grass, his knees sparking mild protest, and put his hand on the leaves, as if to prove the plants existed. He realized his mouth was agape and he tried to set his lips again but found that he was smiling, and it was awkward. And then it wasn't. His wife, God rest her anyway, said he had a wonderful smile, and it wasn't until this morning that he realized he'd been wasting it by hiding it.

He unfolded the note in hand and spread it flat on his knee. The printing was neat, slightly smudged now from being refolded so many times. He read it again, a short paragraph on how to prepare the soil and plant the seeds, and when to water. And then this:

"First: Understand this; creatures are going to come into your garden and take what you grew, often the best of what you grew. You can let it distract you from the beauty, or you can choose to accept it and, if you're wise, to make it part of your intention. You should know that is some of your purpose, to share what you have in your garden.

Second: There will always be weeds. It is your choice to resent their presence and decide how much time you spend dealing with them. If you find you are always pulling weeds, you are working on the wrong thing. I will also tell you that some things you think are weeds bring the most amazing flowers.

Third: Most importantly, you are in charge of what grows in your garden; put there what makes you smile. Plant and grow the things that will be so large, so wonderful, that there will be little room for the weeds, and you will always have enough of the best to share with others. Plant what will fill the garden with what you love, and anyone who sees it will know you."

The man folded the note again and slipped it into his pocket.

Then he raised onto his hands and knees and eased into the garden, pressing the leaves aside, careful not to crush the blueberries he hadn't noticed before. When he was surrounded by the plants, he turned on the damp soil and lay down on his back, arms outstretched into the lush growth.

He felt the earth reach up into him, connecting him to the living things he had planted, the best of him. He felt the light soak into him. He felt his body relax into the soil, the pains fade, and the years dissolve. He laughed for a moment and breathed in the smell of the life around him. And felt himself blooming inside.

Hope this finds you planting,

David

Hope this finds you storytelling

"We tell ourselves stories in order to live."

~ Joan Didion

WE ARE STORIES

December 2014

Greetings from the echo,

"We are lonesome animals. We spend all our life trying to be less lonesome. One of our ancient methods is to tell a story begging the listener to say — and to feel — 'Yes, that's the way it is, or at least that's the way I feel it. You're not as alone as you thought.'" ~ John Steinbeck.

There have been many times, too many to guess the number, where I have told a story in exchange for a place to sleep. Traveling along two-lane roads through farmland or mountain creases or small-town neighborhoods, stopping at a friendly front door. Knocking, telling my story, and waiting to see if I made a connection.

In thousands of miles of travel, I have accumulated stories about these stories. Exchanges of bits of my life for bits of other people's lives, which became a new thing we both walked away with. Our stories.

It is a compelling thing, to share a little of who we are by telling about our family, or how we felt on September 11, or the day our daughter was born, or that time when we almost drowned. We crack open our vulnerability and say what is important, and pray that the listener honors the moment, and perhaps feels the emotion, recognizes it, and empathizes.

We have told stories since the time when they were painted on cave walls. Stories shared around fires of heroic exploits, or family history, or the creation of the world. Prophets, poets, actors, and troubadours traveled from town to town to share stories, some of events from yesterday, some from one hundred years ago, some from tomorrow.

And then we put down words, and created theater, and made radio plays and then movies and vlogs and podcasts. The methods of telling the story fanned out and reached more listeners in different ways, but at the heart of it is someone with an experience they wanted to share.

The things you remember most clearly in your life are bound in emotion. The brain most easily brings back images that are tied to strong emotions: love, excitement, fear, laughter, sorrow. We learn from stories because they connect with emotion for the same reason. When someone shares a vignette from their own life that is laced with strong feelings, it resonates with us and it stays with us.

Sharing the story expresses a glimpse of who we are. Our attitudes about an experience, what we felt in this moment, during that time, after that intersection in our lives. Stories come from what we have observed, what we have learned, how we were changed from an experience.

People love to know these stories. Sometimes for a personal connection or to help them deal with their own demons. Some tales are told only for entertainment, the joy of hearing and the pleasure of telling. Stories can inspire, enlighten, educate, and sometimes they just pass the time when an hour needs to be filled with something other than waiting for the test results.

Our stories are told in how we live our lives too. Those stories are absorbed by our children, our friends, our neighbors, the people who work with us. And the kid you help out of the snowbank, and the woman you hold the door for, and the man you give your coat to. And then that becomes part of their narrative.

I am a writer, a scribe. It is part of my nature now to look for stories, remember them, and add my own spice and then share them. It is a passion of mine, some of which I share here. I love that stories pass through me; my life stories, those I hear from others, some I create that are a mélange of others I have given. It is an honor to be at the crossroads of so many great experiences, just long enough to write them down and share them with others. Some are prompted by the thought, "You should have been there. So let me tell you…"

Something in us wants to tell a story. We need to connect where we have been with what comes next. We want to bring our ancestors with us. We need to teach our children about love. We have to fortify ourselves against a challenge. We remember, we share, and we are made better for it and so are those who witness. And then, inevitably, we need to be known. We exchange the pages of our lives with those whom we meet, and we know that they walk away carrying our immortality, and we bear theirs.

We each have a story to tell. It is how we celebrate that we were here.

Hope this finds you telling yours,

David

MRS. DODGE

February 2001

Greetings from somewhere in time,

The screen door slams open and the little boy storms out into the yard. He stomps down the sidewalk, his feet pounding the Keds onto the pavement in angry slaps. His face is set in an angry frown, his brow furrowed below the severe cowlick that etches his hairline. He marches down the sidewalk, does not look back to see his mother watching him from the door.

He crosses the street, does not stop, look, or listen. He is transfixed in anger. He tromps down the other side of the street, kicking a small rock in front of him. Down the street, past three houses, towards the store to which his mother has sent him.

He is five. His world is toy cars and Lincoln Logs and comic books and crayons. He was deep in this world when his mother gave him the edict to travel one block to the store. Clenched in his fist is a note with a short list and some dollar bills. He has been warned not to lose these.

His pace lessens slightly as he approaches the alley that runs behind the row of stores. He stops at the alley, bends at the waist, and cranes his neck to look down the little road. The older boys in the neighborhood have told him stories of rats that are big as dogs, rats big enough to eat small boys. He hurries across and around the corner to the front of the stores.

He swings open the screen door at Mrs. Dodge's grocery and strides in. He slams the crumpled note and the money on the counter and steps back. His arms are folded on his chest, chin tucked in, and he glares at Mrs. Dodge.

She stands with a broom behind the counter of the small shop, framed by shelves that extend nearly to the ceiling. Cereal boxes, bread, canned goods, jars of pickles form a mosaic behind her. A white apron is stretched across her print dress, there is a pencil wedged in her gray hair, swept up into a bun behind her head. She reaches out to the counter and smooths out the wrinkled note there. She tries a few conciliatory words to the boy, but he is defiant.

Mrs. Dodge packs the few things on the list into a small bag, drops the change in the bottom and slides the bag across the counter. She offers the boy a sucker from the jar on the counter. He shakes his head.

Sliced bread is packaged in cellophane, lined at the bottom with a thin piece of cardboard. Mrs. Dodge slides this liner out of a bag of bread and shows it to the little boy. Printed there is a cartoon rendering of a jolly King, smiling and waving. The boy's countenance cracks. He smiles.

Mrs. Dodge pulls scissors from her apron pocket, frees the little King from the cardboard, and presents it to the little boy. He beams at her. He remembers his manners, and then picks up the bag of groceries and walks out, exchanging goodbyes over his shoulder.

All the way home the boy chats with the King, making the noises and laughs that five-year-old boys make. He announces his arrival at home, brandishes his gift at his mother, and retires to his room. The King is placed in a position of honor, next to his bed.

Weeks later the little boy is in the store with his mother and baby sister. Mrs. Dodge is chatting and sweeping, and the little boy interrupts, expressing a desire for a sucker. His mother chides him for his lack of manners and denies him any candy. The little boy looks to Mrs. Dodge for support, but finds she is allied with his mother. He is betrayed. Tears well in his dark eyes, and he runs out of the store.

He runs past the alley, down the block and across the street to his house, in the front door and to his room. He swipes the King from the bedside and dashes back out of the house. His arms and legs pumping furiously, he runs past his mother on the sidewalk, ignoring her call. Across the alleyway with no glance for monster rats, he careens around the corner to the store.

He bursts into Mrs. Dodge's store and slams the King on the counter. He is breathless from his run, but she knows what he means to say. She looks at his tear-stained face, and she reaches out her hand. He spins around and runs back out.

The little boy and his family move away to another neighborhood. Occasionally they visit, but time eventually erodes their connection with their old neighbors. The boy becomes a young man, not quite so prone to outbursts of defiance. Fourteen summers pass, and one day his picture is in the local paper for some accomplishment. He is handsome, confident, content, smiling out from under his beard. Only a close friend might recognize the little boy that he was once.

And a close friend does. A week after the newspaper article, the young man receives mail from Mrs. Dodge. Inside is a card with a brief note. And folded in a sheet of paper, the King.

The young man travels back to his old neighborhood. He stands in front of his first home, which has been shrunk by time to tiny proportions. He walks down the sidewalk, across the street to the alley. He stands and looks at the trash strewn there and feels no glimmer of fear of rats.

Around the corner, he walks into the store. A man is behind the counter; he eyes the visitor with suspicion. The young man asks for Mrs. Dodge. He is told that she could no longer work in the store. The last time she was robbed, they locked her in the walk-in cooler and scared her into retirement. The young man remembers his manners, and walks out into the summer sun, holding the King in his hand.

Twenty-four summers pass. The young man's cowlick has vanished as his hairline crept away.

All manner of events has swirled around him over time, more good than bad, etching into him the character his parents hoped for when he was born. Happily, his wife saw this potential and did not dismiss him as a defiant boy.

He is surrounded by his children, sitting on the floor of his bedroom, looking through old pictures and letters. Amid the memories, an envelope with his name on it. He empties it on the carpet and there, smiling at him again, is the jolly King from Mrs. Dodge. A reminder of an act of kindness, patience, and of forgiveness. Three strong elements of friendship.

The King is tattered after all his travels, missing the hand that once was his salute. But his smile is there, and the man is reminded of his childhood friend every time he looks at it.

Like I am right now.

Hope this finds you in reverie,

David

FATHER O'MALLEY

April 2019

Greetings from the rookie,

It was about half a mile from the church to Hall Flats, the nearest green space to us where we could practice the various school sports. Hall Flats became either a football field or a baseball field, depending on the season. It was a low place that often flooded, and the houses on the few streets that bordered it were occupied by people who had no other choice.

I was in grade school at St. Matthews Catholic school, a cluster of a few buildings wedged into the downtown city streets where I grew up. There was the church, still a beautiful creation of its sort, now over 100 years old, the rectory, a convent, and the school and gymnasium. What little space was left over on the block it occupied was left as a playground for the students to skin their knees on.

I can still see the high school football players making their way to scrimmage, walking through the busy streets in helmets and pads, clacking their cleats on the sidewalks as Coach Pratt herded them across intersections and past the flower store and the liquor store and down the steps from the bridge into the low field that waited for their blood and sweat.

I know very little about Father J.J. O'Malley. The priests that staffed our church were enigmas, set aside from the daily activities of the school and the cafeteria. They were specters that would be referred to occasionally by Sister Mary Edwin, usually as she administered some corrective advice. We would see them at church services and at sporting events.

Father O'Malley was a compact man, older, whose cleric robes seemed out of place, as if he were a short-order cook disguising himself as a priest. His hair was white and stuck out from under the ball cap he preferred, and tufts of it sprung out from the edge of his t-shirt and at his ears. He was irascible, or at least that was his temperament when he coached the younger teams in basketball and baseball. He was known for his direct language, delivered in short barks, usually seasoned with phrases unlikely common among the clergy.

In church he was a priest, performing his mass with perfunctory form, delivering communion like a blackjack dealer at the edge of the altar. He heard our confessions (sighing at our lack of inspired transgressions, I think) and prescribed our penance with the same lack of inspiration.

Sometimes I would see him behind the rectory, smoking, in his dingy white t-shirt, ill-fitting trousers, scuffed shoes, hunched against the wind, or leaning under the small roof out of the rain, a man waiting for his shift to begin.

Occasionally after basketball practice, he would take a few of us stragglers a couple of blocks over to Kewpies where in those days there was a "Day Old" bakery, and we would be treated to a donut.

It was a gentle gesture in contrast to his impatience with us running "lines" in the gym, or our failure to do the three-man-weave effectively. It was hard to believe it was the same man who would rage at us if we dared walk in street shoes onto the sacred maple court of the St. Matthew's Panthers.

Nearly all my time spent in the company of Father O'Malley was disappointing him, as I was an athlete who did not live up to my potential. In truth, I was comfortable with the arrangement, since in addition to being a lackadaisical competitor, I was a sinner with little success toward redemption. And yet, the one most lasting memory of him was an act of kindness and encouragement. And a lesson in profanity.

We were at Hall Flats practicing baseball. If we ever competed, I don't remember; it seemed all we did was make our way to the Flats, frustrate poor J.J. O'Malley, and then walk back, dirty and discouraged, which quickly led to horseplay in the streets, further raising the ire of the priest.

I was up to bat. I was told to get the bat off my shoulder, to stand in the correct crouch, to keep my eye on the ball. The players in the outfield all moved in, knowing my lack of batting prowess, shouting, "Easy out!" and less complimentary commentary about my abilities.

Father O'Malley, pitching at the moment, turned and roared at the outfield, told them they should be ashamed, that this man was a member of their team, and he was going to shear the leather off the ball, and they would be looking for it for a week. He told them to get to their positions and shut their pie holes. And then he turned to me. If I could have read his mind, I think I would have seen that this is not what he signed up for when he took his vows. If he prayed, it would be for reassignment.

I remember feeling encouraged but still wondering what the hell he was thinking, since I was more likely to hit myself than the ball.

When Father O'Malley delivered the pitch, I swung as hard, and wildly, as my disinterested body would allow.

There are few things as satisfying as the crack of a wooden bat against a baseball, the solid feeling that the connection just made was as God would have wanted it, if he cared about sports. I did not watch the ball for long because my pitcher was telling me to run, Smith, run, and so I did, and before the outfield could recover from watching the ball arc over them, I was on third base. As it happens, I can run.

Father O'Malley walked to third base and clapped me on the shoulder and offered me a word of congratulations. I don't remember what he said exactly because what happened next was more unforgettable. Someone in the outfield had sent the ball back, an impressive throw from right field, perhaps thinking that the third baseman should be in on the play. Which he might have been, had the ball not hit Father J.J. O'Malley squarely in the head, instead.

And that's how I learned the F-word.

If I were writing a screenplay instead of my version of truth, this vignette might be the turning point for our hero. Where, perhaps, because someone saw the natural talent hidden in the young athlete, he gains the confidence to go on to great success in sports, perhaps one day dedicating a home run at Yankee Stadium to the priest who had faith in him. But no. My trajectory in organized sports continued the same uninspired arc downward until I was old enough for people to stop expecting me to play for any other reason than play.

I am grateful to have been involved as I was, and for the enthusiastic (and futile) coaching of people like Father O'Malley. When he finally left our church, for wherever old coach-clerics go when they are put out to pasture, I missed him. I imagine when J.J. made it to his ultimate reward, there was a small celebration for moments like that day on Hall Flats. When I see him again, I'm going to thank him, and let him know I learned more from him than just cussing.

Hope this finds you with your head in the game,

David

BREAKFAST

April 2021

Greetings from the ache,

Not twenty feet from where I sit writing to you, there is a refrigerator filled with food. It faces a pantry that is stocked with every imaginable consumable, and a few I hadn't imagined. This presence is reassuring in a way; I will not go hungry, nor will I ever feel the fear of being hungry. But neither will I take my abundance for granted.

In one of the most influential times of my life, I learned a respect for food. Not as a gourmand or chef, but as a hobo.

Most mornings I woke on the ground, a few feet from my bicycle. I would sit up, the grass damp from dew, and pull things from my saddle bag. Grape-Nuts, sometimes dry from the box, other times soaked in water. I would boil water and make chicory or instant coffee. Sometimes I'd make instant oatmeal, only slightly more appealing than drywall putty. But some mornings, I would pack up my things and ride into the next town and find a diner for breakfast.

I had planned five dollars a day for my existence. The money was mostly for food. I would buy a loaf of bread and a jar of peanut butter, a can of corned beef hash, canned tuna, boxes of noodles. I made it last. And people would give me food. In fact, that was what made the budget possible.

Some days I spent nothing. Some days I had to buy a part for my bike, or a warm shirt, and then for days I would watch every penny. So eating in a restaurant was a luxurious extravagance, and I made the most of it.

I would ride into the town, often a crossroads between farmlands, and then find where the pickup trucks gathered in the first minutes of the day. It would be called "Sweeties" or "Don's" or named after the town, or just called "Diner."

Small towns are as different as fingerprints, but they have things in common. In these little diners, especially as the day started, there was a similar cast of characters. Farmers, local tradesmen, perhaps the constable, all huddling around a meal, trading the news, laughing and gossiping.

In the seventies, it was not unusual to see people packing around the country, but not every place welcomed smelly, long-haired bike bums. So I did my best to be respectful, polite. People would be curious, so I made it easy for them to be.

Sometimes there was a waitress, who would become my ambassador to the rest of the patrons, whispering my story to them as she refilled their coffee. Other times I sat at the counter and the guy cooking would take my order. I looked for whatever breakfast presented the greatest mass of food for the least money. Lots of eggs and potatoes and big slabs of toast, whatever I could fill up on that might carry me through the day. And of course, the bottomless cup of coffee.

I'll also confess I pilfered my share of salt and sugar packets, tubs of jelly, little creamers, wads of napkins. I'm not really ashamed of this now, but I don't suggest it to my children.

In these small spaces, it was natural for people at the next table, or across the room, to ask me things. Where are you headed? How far do you ride a day? What do you do when it rains? Where do you sleep? And if things went well, someone would offer to pay for my meal.

I knew very little about nutrition, only that I was burning a lot of calories every day, and the machine needed to be fed. I was hungry, and some days the space between towns surprised me, so from time to time I ran out of food. Some nights, sleeping under bridges or in cornfields, I would go to sleep still feeling the grumble of my empty stomach.

It's the same ache we have all felt at one time or another, but most of us can solve it easily. In fact, just now I stood up and walked into my kitchen and ate a muffin, answering the mildest mutter of appetite. But there is something that feels desperate and lonely in going to sleep hungry, a pang that I have not forgotten.

Along my way I was fed, literally, by the kindness of strangers. If I stopped at a farmhouse and asked permission to sleep on their land, they invariably would feed me, and send me off the next day with food. A stop at a produce stand, and in exchange for stories of my travels, I would leave with apples or a jar of preserves. People driving past me would stop and give me things. I haven't forgotten these powerful acts of grace.

It has been over four decades since those experiences, and I still feel them as fresh as now. Every time I sit down and order breakfast at a diner, I feel this small rush of gratitude.

Two things remain with me from this passage. First, I will never take a full stomach for granted. Second, I remember the countless times that someone gave me food, or paid for my meal, maybe without knowing what an enormous difference it made. It is one of the simplest ways to help someone else ease an ache. I'm reminded this morning, knowing there are people not far from any of us, whose day can be changed with only the smallest sacrifice of the gift I've been given.

I am going to make my breakfast: a bowl of Grape-Nuts. That thread has stayed with me too.

Hope this finds you sated,

David

REMINDERS

June 2016

Greetings from the adventure,

I still get the same twinge, feel the vibration. When I see a two-lane road split the green in front of me and disappear over a hill. When the road takes me to a place where the world opens up and I can see that it leads to more world.

Forty years ago, on this morning, I awoke in a hammock next to a raging river flowing between thick forests. There was snow on the ground around me and on the mountains above. I was on the lip of Yellowstone, following the road to more world. When I had my coffee and packed up my gear, I swung my leg over the saddle and rode out to find it.

A couple of weeks ago I got a card from my mother. "Happy Fortieth," it said. Took me a few minutes to figure out what anniversary she was remembering. "Keep on spinning," she wrote.

I went to my room and opened a wooden box that sits where I

can see it every morning. Inside are the tattered and stained notebooks from four decades ago. I leafed through the first one and found the date. I had started across the country on my bicycle forty years ago on the date she remembered.

I don't spend a lot of time reminiscing, for good or bad. I love the life I've had, but I love the life I'm living too, so I tend to focus more on this moment than that. And so, it's easy to get surprised by forty years.

I traveled all over the country on my bike, sometimes with friends, sometimes alone. There is no question that those experiences shaped my early life, put grooves in me that would guide many choices since then. That time added color and depth and texture to me that still lives in me.

A lot of what I wrote in those journals was naïve and idealistic and hopeful. Thankfully, a lot of those ideas have stayed with me. I saw, for example, that people are usually generous and open and friendly, and so it was easy to think the best of most everyone I met. That theme has never left me.

I discovered what breathtaking beauty is, not from a screen or through a window, but from being in it. I fought to find words to save what I saw and fell short. Sunrise over the desert. Cruising past the Tetons. Zigzagging along the Pacific Coast. Climbing Trail Ridge Pass over the Rockies. My tires humming on blacktop as I wove between redwoods. In my journal, I tried to describe my impression of the Big Horn Mountains, and like so many times I was at a loss for words. I finally wrote this truth: "…it does not present an image; it is an experience."

Reading my journals, I was reminded …

I would rather be outside. If things are hard, be harder. There is nothing like the sound of rain on your tent. Always treat people like you might meet them later in the day. The mountain does not care.

After a few days without a shower, you're the only person who can't smell you. Coming off the road is hard. It will pass. Being at the mercy of the elements, living in the world and not on it, teaches you humility.

I learned that I could be alone and that there is a price that comes with that. It is good to spend time with yourself, and really face what you think. But from there I gained a new appreciation of what it is like to be with people. Being alone takes practice; there is an ache that gets better, like your body adjusting to a new effort. For me it is a survival skill, not a lifestyle. I love finding people in my day.

Traveling on a bicycle provided a unique connection with the strangers I met every day. They were curious about me, enough to provide us with a place to begin a conversation. That would open doors to a meal, to hospitality, to friendship. I would share what I had, and they would share what they had. It always began with understanding the other's perspective.

I wrote down some reminders of what I thought I would need when the tour ended. Be content. Be where you are. Be patient. "It will pass." Find intensity. Find passion. Be persistent. I can't say I remembered these consistently, but I do recognize the words in some of my days.

The time on the road provided amazing experiences that hold up even after decades of a life filled with amazing experiences. Sleeping on picnic tables, under bridges, in barns, in fields. Grape-Nuts and peanut butter and macaroni and tuna, and coffee and coffee. Riding up mountains, along rivers, and across prairies and into small towns and on to other small towns. Powered by my legs and my determination through deserts and green valleys, past mansions and shacks, through rain and snow and locust swarms and blistering heat. Gas station maps: tracing my finger along the pale gray lines that connected this place with more world. I am sitting at my desk, folding the journals up and putting them back in the box, smiling, grateful for my mother's reminder.

So, I have been sitting here all morning, wondering: what matters in all of this? Maybe it is enough to wade through the memories and enjoy it for what it was, like seeing an interesting movie or reading a book that you enjoy.

But what has been coursing through me since I opened the card from my mom was the thought that forty years from now, I would want to look back at this morning with the same feeling of richness and satisfaction. That this day had been as full as those of my nineteenth year.

Not every day is a mountaintop experience. We have to get the oil changed and do the laundry and wait in line at the DMV. But if we don't build the other stuff into our day, as often as we can, then who will do it for us? Who else will make this the day that will shine through the next forty years? To be honest, that is the most important lesson I brought off the road, one that I have forgotten too often.

"There are as many worlds as there are kinds of days, and as an opal changes its colors and its fire to match the nature of a day, so do I." ~ John Steinbeck, *Travels with Charley*

Hope this finds you swinging your leg over the saddle,

David

STEEL

July 2011

Greetings from where I forge it,

I met Team Hoyt on the course of the Boston Marathon and saw it firsthand. Dick Hoyt has pushed his quadriplegic son in a wheelchair through hundreds of marathons, duathlons, triathlons, and even a trek across the United States. It is an amazing story of dedication and determination. Dick is 70 years old.

He has steel.

There is a moment in our decisions, the place where we choose to give in, give up, give out, or we choose to try harder, to overcome, to prevail. It is a moment of courage and determination, followed by another and another until the choices make the difference we desire. It is when you reach deep, past the convenient and the usual. It is where you find the steel.

The steel is refined by challenges. As someone once said, "The finest steel has to go through the hottest fire." In order to use it, we have to learn from what happens to us and push out from what we have thought we are capable of, to find what we can really do.

I am not simply talking about answering a physical challenge. We reach for the steel in all aspects of our life. It is your integrity in the face of the hard decision. When the doctor calls you to say he has bad news, and he has bad news. When you are down to your last ten dollars and looking at a stack of bills. When your wife of fifty years no longer knows your face.

When you face the same pain or loneliness day after day and struggle to find hope, and the words roll in your head as you try to sleep: "Why me? When will it get better?" And you know you must shake it off, pull from somewhere in you the resolve to push past what will ruin you to what will make you.

And then you find the steel. You choose what you will and not what you are given.

Like not giving up on a dream even when you don't know how to take the first step, even when the statistics tell you to go sell insurance instead, even when the loudest voices shout down your best idea and what you really want to do is put it away and not face it again. And then you try anyway because that's what you are made of.

One of the satisfying things about running a marathon is testing the limits and finding there is more. And asking for more of yourself when you are past your capacity, past remembering why you are doing what you're doing. One lesson that comes from that experience: if I can do this, what else might I do? Because if I can find the steel in that simple act of running, I can find it whenever I need it.

I have met Olympic athletes, politicians, astronauts, and cancer survivors. I have met authors and artists and singers and actors. I have met parents and entrepreneurs, teachers and doctors and recovering alcoholics. In all of these, I have looked closely and known they have steel. I don't have to see them tested to know they have it. They don't have to show it to prove they have it.

Some gather it from their faith, others from the support of friends. Some find it in their own experience or the example of others. Some hear it in music or find it in meaningful prose. Some find it in love. Some find it in hate. But it is inside us, brought to the surface by whatever means we choose.

Yes, there are some in the world who never reach for it, never find it, though I think we are all given the steel. There are those who become so accustomed to the easy way or who have never seen how challenges can be overcome that they are helpless to call on the strength when the extraordinary is required.

When I was young, about to leave on a bike tour, a friend gave me a T-shirt with the letters "IF" on it. It was to remind me that IF I needed strength, I had it: Intestinal Fortitude. Guts. Grit. It is determination, courage, twisted together with a personal discipline. These are the cables of steel in us all. It is the resolve that allows us to choose to not give in to the doubt, the fear, and defeat.

Mohandas Gandhi said, "Strength does not come from physical capacity. It comes from an indomitable will."

This force of will in humans is what keeps us reaching. It is why we write books, run marathons, choose life, take risks, and try again. It is what separates the life we want from the life that sometimes appears before us.

I sit down and arrange these words each week for a variety of reasons. I write for the friends I have on the other side of these pages. I write for my own pleasure, to sort my own thoughts, and on some Mondays, to look for the steel.

Hope this finds your mettle tested,

David

LETTER FROM ALEXANDER

March 2022

Greetings from the other side,

Dear Dad,

I got your message yesterday, and I've been thinking about ways to respond so you know I'm paying attention and that I am with you all. I don't want it to be awkward, but this will need to be our secret since usually our prayers for you there are intended to be more subtle.

I was there yesterday as you celebrated our birthdays, felt your joy and heard the laughter, saw the gifts. And then in that quiet moment, in between, I heard you say what you always do, and I answered in the only way I am able.

In truth, you already see my responses, although some mornings you don't know it, since you are aware of so many things for other reasons. But I was there in the wild of the murmuration, and in the velvet, darkness giving way to the crease of cameo rose, the sound of the small creek singing between the rocks where you pause to say good morning.

One day you will tell them about this, but I've been with my brothers, watched them, and felt them as they make their way. I grow as they grow, feel heartache and happiness, sense frustration and hope. Even from where I watch the world unfold, where there is only light, I know what life feels like there. Shadows, cold starlight, brilliant sun, the warmth of the perfect afghan, rain sluicing on windows. I know.

Something I have been excited to share with you has to do with prayer. They seem to come in all colors, from the petition, to praise, to simple conversation. And sometimes they are acts of love, which from here are like a kind of music. Most often we hear these as whirling swirls of sound; they seem to be with us all the time, like the morning greetings of birds.

What is especially beautiful is when I hear a prayer, or a thought from one of you, that is meant for me personally. I want you to know about this, somehow, because our prayers for you all arrive in a similar way. Aunt Leslie says it feels like you are remembering something special, that's how it comes to you. I think it's like when you get a new idea, that sensation of light in your chest, and the realization of an original thought in your mind.

It will be different for each of you, but I think the sensation is similar. When we send a prayer it may seem like a fleeting thought. Some days you remember a wisp of a dream, or you pause for what you think is déjà vu. I'm smiling at that, knowing you all feel us, know we are praying for you.

There are so many other things for us to talk about, and we will in time. But for now, I simply wanted you to understand that I know you all wonder, and sense my absence, and I know the moments you feel sadness, feel loss. And those moments share the same space as the joy and beauty of your lives.

There are some things I shouldn't share, those mysteries that need to remain as such. I know you respect this, and that's the way you'd want it. But I want you to carry a message for me.

Tell Sawyer not to doubt his passions, and that he was right; I got to have a dog, and I am the luckiest. Harrison should know that his kindness is felt far more than he knows, and I laugh at almost everything he thinks is funny. Get word to Carson that we smell the bread, and we feel his acts of service, and hope grows in the world. And Katherine, who would be my friend and sister, whose life radiates out in her children, let her know that their future is brilliant, and her love continues for ages. Tell Mom that there was never pain, except when I first knew I would be apart from you all, and that all changed in a moment to something so glorious that words are too poor to say.

Of course, you can't simply tell them, any more than I can. But I trust you, and I know you will find a way of sharing this all without letting anyone know our secret. The time will come when we can sit with coffee, elbows on the table, and share whatever passes in this time apart. Until that moment, love that sweet world, know I hear your prayers, and I am sending mine.

Your grateful son,

Alexander

Hope this finds you praying,

David

HENRY

July 2020

Greetings from the messengers,

God has a friend named Henry.

When Henry was grown up, God sent him a message, which he didn't get, and so he sent him several more, all of which were missed. Finally, God lifted him from his little village, and they had a long talk. From that day on the two of them were lifetime friends. Which means a lot when you consider it.

Henry caught God's attention because of the way he prayed, which always included questions, and, strangely, laughter. Henry was not a devout man; he had his frailties, but there was a peace about him that drew people to him. He was kind, and above all, he was a good listener. Plus, he had a great laugh.

When Henry first met God, it was awkward, of course, but over time he grew comfortable with having coffee with the Creator of the universe. After a while, Henry realized that he had been chosen, at first as a prophet, which didn't work out, and then as a messenger of a different sort.

"What do I call you? I mean, I feel like I should say Mr. Something, or Your Majesty. You know?" Henry asked. God thought this was funny, and reminded Henry that people used many names, from many faiths and beliefs. "Don't get too twisted up in formalities. We've known each other a long time."

Every so often God would ask Henry to visit Earth. Henry would walk around and listen to people, get a feel for what they were feeling and thinking. He would stand in lines with them, ride subways, bale hay, do grocery shopping. One summer he stayed in an internment camp in California, another time in a sweatshop in New York. For a while, he lived in a Māori village and learned all manner of beautiful words, which he memorized to tell God.

When he sat with God later, Henry would describe what people were doing and use the words they used. Henry was very good at expressing the feelings of the people he met because they were imprinted on him. He understood them because he listened and wanted to understand.

Henry would dare to go anywhere there were people to listen to. Henry listened to people who were in hospice, he listened to people working in factories, listened to the homeless, the desperate, the prisoners, the addicts. He listened to the people who were afraid to pray or didn't for other reasons. He listened and asked simple questions. And in between, he laughed with people.

Some days he listened to children exclusively because it was refreshing.

Henry visited with everyone, and he was everyone. Henry was a Masai hunter, an Irish peat farmer, a woman in a refugee camp, a hairdresser in Brooklyn, a politician in Colombia. He marched with protestors in Biloxi, in Tiananmen, and he stood near barbed wire at borders, in prisons, and in drug houses. He worked on a farm for a few years and heard about raising crops and raising children. He listened to the corn.

For generations he listened, and then came back and sat with God and told him what people said and felt. God said: "What are they afraid of?" And Henry said: strangers, death, snakes, going hungry, being forgotten. Sometimes You. "What makes them happy?" Loving and being loved. Chocolate. Living an interesting life. Creating things. Sometimes You.

Henry knew that God already had these answers, but somehow it was good to hear them out loud. And then they would visit, elbows on the table, steaming mugs of coffee in front of them.

And God would talk to Henry. He told him about apteryx and black holes and how science and religion both are sometimes disappointing. He told him about how time really passed, and how hard it was to watch people suffer. He told him the secret of light. Some days it was simple things like laundry, and other days it was harder things like the lost sheep. But what Henry realized was that God just liked having him to talk to. He really was a good listener.

Henry brought the messages back from the people he listened to and listened while God sifted through things and asked the questions. One day Henry asked God if he was ever lonely. God laughed, which he did often when they were together. "No, Henry, why would you ask that?" Henry was a little self-conscious, but said, "I just wonder how you feel when I'm not here."

God said, gently, "Henry, you are not the only one I send to listen."

Hope this finds you listening,

David

BLUE HERON

August 2019

Greetings from the confluence of awe,

The ditches along the country roads are deep with rainwater. The reeds have filled up the low place between the road and the field, taller than normal because it's too wet to cut them. Here is where rabbits wait to be released into the mad dash across the tarmac, where yellow finches dart and swoop.

I ran a few feet from the edge of this, lost in thought, watching the road come to me, running effortlessly, sweating in the morning sun. My thoughts were floating as easily as I did, moving through the miles.

In this moment, from a low place, a catch basin at the edge of a field where the culverts come together, suddenly there was this glorious movement. Out of the reeds came a phoenix, graceful and impossibly slow against the pull of gravity, stretching into the first feet above the tips of the grasses. A Great Blue Heron flowed into the air, opening its wings to a six-foot span, a beautiful, powerful display of movement and color. She crushed space around her, folding the tips in as she surged up, and then captured the air again and pushed into the sky.

I was held in awe, too amazed to even be startled. The heron was facing me, wings fully open, pointing its long beak up, and then turned in the blue background and swept again and rushed higher away from us mere earthbound mortals.

For a mile or two after this encounter, I remained in a state of amazement. I held on to the image of this incredible example of life that happened just inches from where my own was taking place.

Ahead of me, clouds of gnats were held in place by the sun, their tiny wings glistening in the light as they swirled together in a choreography nature wrote before I existed. It is something that is easy to miss, or to take for granted, but I had just been taught a lesson from the heron. *See it, David. It is a miracle you are here in this moment.*

The thought came to me, not in words but images, that as I gave witness to these things, as they happened right in front of me, I happened right in front of them. I was a miracle for them. I say this with the full knowledge of my frail, fractured existence, knowing that I only can be here out of the graciousness of my Creator, and it is still true; I am a miracle too.

For each person whom you meet today, whether you think you planned it or the moment is serendipitous, the cumulation of actions that make the exchange possible is remarkable. Look at that person with all of that and be in awe. Oh, and by the way, they should be in awe of you. Not only because you both exist in that same moment, but because of everything that is in you and them that made it possible. It is fantastic. The potential is even more inspiring.

Somewhere on a lonely road a heron waits, thinking heron

thoughts. A couple of hours before, I sat on the lip of my deck, the first cup of coffee in my hand, watching the day come. The hint of light in the inky sleep of night, the peach-rose blush, the first taste of the richness of the day coming my way. I don't think too hard about these things; it is an instinct of mine to be there as the day shows its passion. I am never disappointed.

I dawdled and stretched and retied my shoelaces and rethought my route and took a hundred other actions that filled the seconds and minutes before I took my first step. Miles later, not a coincidence, but the perfect unfolding of living, I met a heron. And she met me.

Some weeks ago, before Summer staked its claim, I was in the garage, and I saw something moving on the door going into the house. I looked closer and it was a circle of white, and inside there was a movie of leaves dancing. After a few minutes of searching, I found where the sunlight was focused through a tiny nail hole in the flashing of the outside wall. Beyond that was a maple tree, its new leaves waving to me in the morning light, now projected on the inside door.

The sun was only in that place for a moment, passing over a hole so small I would never know its existence otherwise. Its trajectory in the day, as our planet rotates, and its path in the year as we roar around the sun was a miraculous confluence of timing. Add to that I was there to witness it, which, with the thousands of variations that could happen that morning, might not have been true. I was there to see what played out, and all of existence around me was there to witness me as well.

The moments that pile up in your day that lead to the next intersection of you and beauty, or whatever waits for you, are a convergence so incredible that they will likely never be repeated in all of time, and since they occur, they will be true for all of time. It is fantastic.

I did not know the experience of the heron or the gnats or rabbits or the sun before I crossed paths with any of them. I think there are a billion variations that might have led us to intersect in a different way. But that morning they existed as they did, and the heron rose out of the grasses and was amazed at a man passing by. Graceful and powerful, glistening in the morning sun, floating along the road as if he owned it, moving across the earth away from mere feathered mortals. The heron rose into the sky in awe of me and was changed for all of its existence.

Hope this finds you in awe of you,

David

CHAPTERS

July 2014

Greetings from the next chapter,

The man walked in short strides to match his companion, the little girl walking next to him, tilting just a fraction so that he could hold her hand. They walked down the hallway to the library, and he paused to open the door for her and bowed slightly, ushering her into the room.

The sun filtered in through the slats of the blinds, casting gray rectangles on the wood floor. Bits of dust traced through the light, tiny specters drifting toward a place to rest.

She looked around, curious. She couldn't really remember spending time in this room, even though the doors were always open. Today it was like it was brand new, as if it had just been created at the end of the hall while she was out playing.

The desk was a simple table, a few things scattered there as if someone just stood up from writing something. A small clock ticked softly, nested between pictures.

The walls were lined with library shelves stained a deep chestnut, reaching almost to the ceiling, interrupted only by the windows looking out into the woods. Each shelf was filled with books, a myriad of colors, their spines lined up in an uneven picket. Like every library, the books seem to hum in anticipation of the next reader.

She absently twisted one finger through a lock of hair, one of two braids draped on her shoulders. "Ummm . . ." she said to herself, looking around to see what things might be interesting to girls of her age.

The man sat in the desk chair and swiveled to face her and swept a yellow book off the desk as he turned. He watched her taking in the room, turning, mouth slightly open, staring at the shelves. He absently flipped the pages of the book, bits of ribbon and papers jutting from the pages marking where he had been reading. He glanced at a page and smiled, then closed it and slid it onto the desk, precisely where it had been waiting.

"What are all these ... books?" she asked. "Are they yours? Did you read them all?"

He smiled and waited for her to look back at him. "You could say that. I have read them all because I have written all the words in them." The man sat in the desk chair and leaned on his knees so he could look his daughter in the eyes. He smiled at her.

She looked at him, digesting what he said, trying to puzzle it out, part of her checking to see if he was teasing her. He took a deep breath.

"These books are about all the people I have met. Everyone that has come into my life. It is a library of people."

She gasped. "Everyone? It's a lot of books." She paused. "It's so many books, it makes me a little dizzy." She held her arms out as if to steady herself as she tipped her head back to look at the highest shelves.

He laughed lightly. "Some people are only a few pages. Others fill up chapters. Some people, the important ones, take many books. Volumes and volumes."

Her eyes widened.

"Everyone you EVER met?" Her math skills failed her.

"Well, not quite. Everyone I have come to know."

"It's just that you are … you have been alive a long time and that would be a lot of people."

He could see her mind whirling, trying to piece together what he said with the books that surrounded them. "I have been alive a long time. But some people are just in my life for a season. Some for years and years. Some people will be in my life forever. So, there are different sizes of books for each of them."

She seemed to make sense of that and relaxed her face a little. "Why? Why do you write these books about the people?"

"Different reasons. Mostly because they mean something to me, and I want to create a way of expressing that." He pressed his lips together, thinking. "Sometimes when I miss someone, I can take the book out and go back and enjoy our time together. I can look at the words they said or how they made me feel." He leaned back in the desk chair. "It is a little like having them with me whenever I wish."

The girl smiled. She liked the sound of his voice in here. She began to feel the warmth from the shelves around them. Because she was a reader, she felt the words call to her.

Her father turned in the chair and reached for a thin book bound in mahogany leather. He split the pages and placed his fingers on a page.

"This is about someone I knew for a little while, a long time ago, when I was your age. Maybe you'll see what I mean." He drew a breath and read the words:

"He swings open the screen door at Mrs. Dodge's grocery and strides in. He slams the crumpled note and the money on the counter and steps back. His arms are folded on his chest, chin tucked in, and he glares at Mrs. Dodge.

She stands with a broom behind the counter of the small shop, framed by shelves that extend nearly to the ceiling. Cereal boxes, bread, canned goods, jars of pickles form a mosaic behind her. A white apron is stretched across her print dress, there is a pencil wedged in her gray hair, swept up into a bun behind her head. She reaches out to the counter and smooths out the wrinkled note there. She tries a few conciliatory words to the boy, but he is defiant.

Mrs. Dodge packs the few things on the list into a small bag, drops the change in the bottom and slides the bag across the counter. She offers the boy a sucker from the jar on the counter. He shakes his head.

Sliced bread is packaged in cellophane, lined at the bottom with a thin piece of cardboard. Mrs. Dodge slides this liner out of a bag of bread and shows it to the little boy. Printed there is a cartoon rendering of a jolly King, smiling and waving. The boy's countenance cracks. He smiles."

The man looked over the book at the girl. "Books sometimes are like the people in our lives," he said, idly thumbing the pages in his hand. "Some are your favorite. You know them almost by heart. Others you read when you need a laugh or to think deeply about things. Some are just … people you meet, maybe you don't always know what they will mean in your life. You just keep turning the pages to find out."

He put the book back, tracing his fingers along other books, over a bright green binding, working it free from the shelf. There were dozens of bookmarks tucked in the pages. He thumbed through it, smiling, and put it on the shelf. For a moment he forgot himself until he saw his daughter staring, waiting to ask a question. He slid the book back home.

He sat in the chair again and gathered her into his lap. She put her hand on his shoulder and got comfortable.

"What is it you want to ask?" he said.

"Are there books about my brothers?"

"Yes of course." He watched her, anticipating the next question.

She turned her head and looked back at him, then looked away. "Is there a book about me?" she asked a little shyly, now studiously examining her fingertips.

He laughed and she felt the vibration from his chest. "Of course. I have written about you every day of your life." He set her down and stood up and moved to another section of shelves. She took his place in the chair and crossed her ankles, swinging her feet idly back and forth, rocking the chair gently.

He opened a book. He touched his thumb to his tongue and turned a few pages.

"My daughter Katherine is someone you would like to know. She is friendly and outgoing, but unless you are watching closely, you might not see what I am about to describe. She lives in the self-assured, quiet manner of someone who may not have everything figured out but is at ease with the process of learning. That sometimes disguises how passionate she is about her life.

Katherine is compassionate and smart and friendly and fun. And those of you who have read about her here already know, she has Steel. A strength that runs through her that carries her through challenges and setbacks and detours, to where her fullest potential lies."

She wriggled in the chair. "That's about me?" she asked, with a nervous giggle.

"It is, and it will be," he said to her.

She glanced away, her eyes roaming over the shelves again.

"What are those books there?" she asked, pointing to the next shelf.

He smiled and didn't say anything right away. He looked at her and then back at the books. He coaxed a book from the shelf. It was bound in cloth, heavily textured, in heathered tones of wheat and green and bits of coral. He held the book flat between his hands. He looked at her, thinking about what he wanted to say.

"In your life you will have many friends, because you are such a treasure," he said. His daughter smiled shyly, watching his eyes and glancing at the book he held.

"Some friends will be for a time, and some for a lifetime. And one day you will meet someone whose friendship will become more than that. He will be someone you care about deeply, and who cares as deeply for you."

She shifted in her seat, curious. Her eyes, wells of ocean blue, searched him.

"This book will be about that person. Someone we haven't met yet, but about whom I am very much looking forward to writing." He smiled at her. "Because I know you, I feel like I'll know him."

She reached out tentatively to touch the book, looked at her father, arching her eyebrows and asking permission. He let her take the book and watched her turn it in her hands.

She ran her hands over the cloth binding and looked at the spine, then gently eased the front cover open. She slipped her fingers under the cover page and laid it flat so she could see the first page.

He watched her. Her eyes roamed over the page, and her lips shaped the word as she said it to herself.

"Daddy?"
"Yes?"
"Who is 'Tim'?"

Hope this finds you reading again,

David

ILA BIRD

April 2020

Greetings from the nest,

Katherine told us that the nuthatch will take bits of leaves or insects and scurry around the opening to the nest in the tree, sweeping the surface of the bark. The purpose, it turns out, is to throw predators off the scent of her nest. It was one of those little things I would never have bothered to understand, and it was a beautiful gift to know.

We sat in the sun, my wife and I, about six feet and a generation away from our granddaughter Ila Rose. She was tucked inside a blanket, making little songs, or perhaps poems, the rhymes of which none of us could guess.

It was a month since we last held her, just after she was born, which was both moments and eons ago. Since then, because of quaranine, we have had her image, but not the warmth and weight of her. There is an ache in holding a baby for a long time, and there is an ache in not holding her for a long time.

The bird scurried up and down the tree, making light scratching noises on the bark. I looked up at the sound, watched her for a moment, dancing along the tree's shape, admired the nimble energy, the sureness of movement. I thought how lucky she is to be able to fly.

A few weeks ago, we drove the hour or so to their home to bring food and a few things that new parents would want and saw Ila through the glass. It was a peculiar experience, one I was not prepared for, as if anything would prepare us. I was grateful to have seen Katherine and Tim holding Ila, but drove home feeling like I'd been to a strange exhibit of my family.

The nuthatch will stand in the opening of the nest and spread her wings. She will do a little ballet there, appearing as fierce and imposing as a tiny bird can, sending a brave image to squirrels or other raiders that she is not to be trifled with. It is a graceful and powerful movement, a tiny, colorful flutter of poetic drama.

We sat on the deck on an almost ordinary Saturday afternoon, and the conversation pushed past the strangeness of waiting in line for an hour to enter the grocery store and the comically elusive toilet paper. Until we were talking about normal things, and baby things, and simple treasures. Ila squirmed and settled and then napped, a skill I admired, and recognized as one inherited from me.

I looked up and saw the nuthatch was watching us. She seemed still, framed in the nearly perfect circle of her home. I don't know what she made of our arrangement, our shifting and swaying, the little noises we made back and forth. The way we held and protected our Ila Bird.

Stories have floated into my day, of people separated from those they love, sometimes in tragic moments, in heartbreaking experiences. I know these stories sear and scar the lives around us.

By contrast, our tableau, a sunny afternoon, separated by mere feet and not lifetimes, is one to be grateful for.

This slip of time, one of worry, of shortages, of sickness, and uncertainty, of death, is a pale echo of times the world has suffered through. But it is real enough, challenging enough, in some small ways, in some more lasting ways. One truth I have kept with me since I was old enough to understand, words that might keep us humble in good times and hopeful in trying times: All Things Pass.

A year from now Ila will be walking, already exploring the world in her way. Every new thing a brilliant discovery, each bump a surprise, each new color a delight. This time of separation, of limitations, will be nothing to her, other than perhaps stories someone will tell one day.

We are told not to worry, that if God is watching over even the tiniest bird in the forest, the simplest flower, you know His eye is on us as well. I'll admit I've struggled with this message, wondering. But that's our place in life: to wonder.

The nuthatch, by nature, is in almost constant motion. Foraging, feeding, protecting, fleeing, seeking love, adapting. She moves almost constantly; it is her way of surviving and being sure those she loves have the chance to thrive.

And yet she stood still in the dark round space, the door of her nest, and watched us. The symmetry of the moment startled me. And this morning this other thread appeared, this feeling that the same Creator who watches over the tiniest bird may send her to watch over our Ila Bird. She who dances and sweeps, she who is grace and power and courage, hovers in care over the one who needs her.

In each life there are signs and messages; some we are open to, some are given and explained, and others are left for us to unwrap when we are ready.

I know as I sit watching this day lighten that not far from here the nuthatch spreads her wings wide, holds them apart as if to embrace the day, and then slowly pirouettes, brave guardian over our sleeping treasure. In opening her wings, in sharing that color and shape, she makes herself more than she is, to give care for the one who still makes rhymes in her dreams.

"'Hope' is the thing with feathers -/That perches in the soul - " ~ Emily Dickenson.

Hope this finds you lifted on wings,

David

Hope this finds you celebrating

*"There are only two ways to live your life.
One is as though nothing is a miracle.
The other is as though everything is a miracle."*

~ Albert Einstein

FOR GOODNESS SAKE

December 2012

Greetings from over the river,

My Dad is driving the Buick, gripping the steering wheel, wrestling the machine, willing the four tires to stay in the two black slots carved in the snow in front of us. The windshield wipers are whipping back and forth, cutting half ovals in the snow on the glass.

The car is hot, the heater blowing at maximum hellfire to fight back the fog of our breathing on the windows and melt the ice and snow outside. The powder whirls around us as the car barrels along the vague outline of the road. There are no other cars; it is Christmas Eve, already dark, and other families are already observing the curfew. Our headlights broadcast in front of us as if to emphasize our singular defiance.

We are driving the two-lane road that cuts through the farmland south of our town, the twenty-mile space that separates the city mice and the country mice. I press my face against the glass, watching the houses go by, a few of them with lights on the porch, my five-year-old mind marshaling my limited attention span on one thing.

I am in the back seat, loosely packed in with various wrapped gifts along with my sisters. One is old enough to torment me, the other too young for me to torment. I am trapped by circumstance and the pressure of Being Good, imposed by an omniscient elf somewhere north of us.

When I become bored, I crawl up into the package shelf, wedge myself against the rear window of the car. In some other circumstance my Dad might have commented about being able to see out the back, but the windows are frosted by the snow and there are no cars behind us, so I am spared.

I climb down into the seat again, pushing up to the door, toying with the little ashtray lid built into the upholstery, flipping it open and letting it snap shut until the noise becomes irritating enough to elicit a comment from the front seat where my mother sits. The car windows are steamed up and I draw circles in the condensation, making stick figures running across the glass. They dissolve before the piece is complete, running in drips down to the edge of the door.

When we reach the village where my grandparents live, the gas station is closed, and the few shops are dark. Only the flashing yellow signal at the intersection offers any suggestion that people have not completely abandoned this remote place.

We turn down the narrow road to my grandparents' house, a risky maneuver; but the snow is no match for the Buick. We blow up white clouds as we plow down the little road and turn into the long driveway, already crowded with powder-covered cars. The four doors open and we spill out, children and parents and packages and bags. I am hurrying through the shallow snow to the front door, wanting this to be done as fast as possible, my mind on that one thing. The sooner I am in bed and asleep, the sooner Santa will come.

My grandparent's living room is crowded with people. Some are my relatives, some are neighbors; I stop trying to figure out who is who. There are lots of kisses, starting with my Grandma's, leaving crimson tattoos from the latest Avon red. The air is thick with perfume and cigarette smoke.

There is loud talking and laughter as we listen to the Vaughan Meder album about the Kennedy family at Christmas. I only vaguely understand why this is so funny, and laugh along with the adults, hoping that if I participate, we can finish this sooner.

I am polite, but after a while I am too tired to keep up pretenses. Even the pressure of Being Good falters, and I find myself losing interest in the adult questions about how old I am or what Santa might bring me. Just the reminder of Santa quickens my heart, and I am impatient to get home to complete the sequence required for him to appear.

The rooms are small, more crowded with a Christmas tree now, and a few extra chairs pulled in for company to sit in. I maneuver through knees, exploring little dishes on the tables trying to find chocolate, but Grandma's treats are taffy and ribbon candy. I frown but remember to Be Good and put a hard candy in my mouth to show my selfless spirit.

There is a TV in the corner, but it is only turned on for boxing or the news. Now the hi-fi is playing Christmas music. I can sense Santa's impatience, almost feel him drumming his fingers on the edge of his sleigh, waiting to take off but held in place by me. He knows when I am sleeping and knows when I'm awake. And I'm awake.

The pre-Christmas tension is almost too much. The children are given token gifts to open, but it seems as though they are like apples at Halloween. Practical things like pajamas and underwear, as if we needed more of those, as if no one had ever asked a child what they wanted for Christmas. I smile, holding up another pair of white socks with the little stripes around the top, giving my most earnest impression of Being Good. "Look!" I say, projecting Academy Award-winning enthusiasm, as if I had just received a G.I. Joe or a Matchbox car.

The evening stretches out into infinity and I am chafing in my good clothes, fidgeting under the pressure of Being Good, and finally my resolve cracks. I want to go home, and somehow being subtle is not working. I express my impatience and am warned and reminded about the rules. I sit in insolence in the corner by the tree, shielded by the fir, my hot tears burning my eyes, roiling in five-year-old angst, knowing that the reindeer will not pull the sleigh until I have lived up to my responsibility.

Finally, mercifully, the time ends, and we are bundled up and kissed again and sent out into the polar breeze with a new set of gifts traded for those we brought. We crowd into the car, shivering on the vinyl seats, begging for the Buick to warm up.

My Dad urges the car down the snowy roads, surrounded by dark, the landscape dotted with the occasional house light, a few doors lighted with colorful bulbs, a few Christmas trees visible from picture windows. I don't know if it is a hundred miles or a thousand, but we cannot drive fast enough for the time to pass as I hope it will.

Before long the car is warm and my Dad turns on the radio, the volume low so we can just make out the strains of Bing Crosby dreaming. I peer between the seats at the dash lights, a cozy glow against the blackness outside the windows. I lean against the door, letting the warmth soak into me, wrapped in my winter coat and hat, my anxiety lessened now that we are pointed in the right direction. Surely Santa will see I'm making an effort.

The car pushes on through the dark, toward the big city where we live. The drone of the car and the soft crooning combine to lull me, and the heat makes me drowsy. I close one eye, just for a moment, and feel the pull of sleep, inexorable, a weight on me that I am powerless against. I drift for a moment. And the world changes.

And then I am somewhere, a room filled with toys, my heart racing as I open a gift, and another, and here is a stocking filled with chocolate, and then I am being carried, I am vaguely aware I am outside again, and I see our front door, the little fire truck over the porch, and then I am next to the Christmas tree, and look at all the gifts, wrapped in red and green, and now I am in my bed, magically clothed in my pajamas. I ask if I am Being Good and am assured that I am. The pronouncement is ratified with a kiss just below my cowlick.

I smile and turn on the pillow, and in my five-year-old mind I sense the release, the moment when I am synchronized with Santa, when he knows he can snap the reins and begin the journey. He knows when I am sleeping.

Hope this finds you Being Good for Goodness' Sake,

David

CATHEDRAL OF TREES

September 2020

Greetings from the congregant,

When I was a couple of years shy of twenty and traveling around the country, I woke up in the middle of the night in a field in Wyoming surrounded by nothing but horizon. Above me was a sky overflowing with stars, densely packed constellations, whorls and ribbons of living light. The earth was dark and the sky was alive with creation, with brilliant mystery.

It was not the first time or the last that I was treated to such a sight; most of us have had some similar experience, but on that night, it came with the indelible, undeniable presence of the Creator. It was a powerful moment, alive in overwhelming beauty. Even now, decades later, I feel a shiver, not only of awe but of synchrony.

I have been in churches all my life, in various levels of engagement. I have been inspired there, been humbled, been bored, found reasons to forgive and to ask for grace. I have had conversations with God, usually somewhat formal, aligned with whatever was the order of worship. These are part of my faith life, but what I want to share with you is a separate thing that matters to me.

Yesterday I ran in the vestiges of summer, a warm sunny morning. I zigged my way through town, scattering errant leaves here and there, joining the river on a path into the woods. Geese laughed overhead, not clear yet on their direction, making wide circles over the forest.

I wasn't thinking about running; that was more instinctual, as was my direction. It was not a new route; I could find my way without concentrating, and that can open things up for me.

I have been in churches of all varieties and faiths, from modest adobe structures or open-air sheds to the most magnificent structures built to honor God. The Basílica de la Sagrada Família in Barcelona, the Cathedral of Santa Maria del Fiore in Florence, Old South Church in Boston, St. Louis Cathedral in New Orleans, our own St. Matthews where I grew up. You don't have to look them all up; trust me, this is an impressive church resume. The construction of many of these works of art took generations to complete. It was rare that anyone alive for setting the foundation would be there for the dedication. Nothing I have to say takes anything away from these places, my experiences there, their history, or their purpose.

I ran along the river, aware now that some of the trees were already pulling on fall fashion. Crisp remnants were scattered along the path, walnuts plopped to the earth in dull thuds. The trees creaked a melancholy song in the light breeze as if they were reluctant to see the sun in its new place, now just over the horizon.

Frank Lloyd Wright said, "I believe in God, only I spell it 'nature.'" Some in my world might frown at this, cast pagan aspersions on the sentiment. Whatever his intent was, I like having the words. I know that Wright's work sought to bring man and nature together in harmony, both God's creations, but too often separated by architecture and by civilized thinking.

I left the river and clambered up a steep hill, carved with roots for steps, and then ran up a dirt path into the woods. The trees crowded close enough to touch as I wove higher along the bluff, deeper into the forest. I looked down over the trees that framed the river, deep greens with patches of orange and red. A heron glided over the water, unaware I was watching from above.

I stopped at a fallen tree and leaned on its bark, felt the sweat run down my skin, my heart hammering in my chest, the air filling my lungs, and felt the world settle around me. John Burroughs said he went to nature "to be soothed and healed, and have my senses put in order." I could feel that settle on me, far enough into my run to have sweated out the distractions I woke up with. I turned to go back down the path toward home and instead was taken to church.

I have felt God in peculiar places. In emergency rooms, on a Greyhound bus, in chance encounters with people, in narrow escapes from fatal moments. I once took Wonder Bread communion from the back of a tattered pick-up truck, standing next to a small cemetery in the middle of South Dakota, and it was one of the most satisfying moments in my faith life. I have been in a tent, in a mechanic's bay, in an abandoned shed, and regardless of what the place was meant for, it contained the Creator.

And so it was yesterday. I saw a shaft of sunlight piercing the trees, lighting the narrow path in another direction. I turned that way and ran under the canopy of the forest, dodging roots and rocks. A deer trotted with me in the shadows. The sun turned the trees into a cathedral, brilliant stars of light between the green places, lighting up the autumn colors, deep orange and burgundy and yellow, stained glass among the maples and oaks. Brilliant columns of sunlight stood among the trees, changing the earth and wood and leaves into a sanctuary, an adytum, a tabernacle, a place of peace where God is present.

In any ordinary moment there can be a miracle. It happens to us when we are not paying attention, these holy exchanges between people or among any of creation. In those places God exists, and whatever your beliefs, doctrines, whatever your religion, you can connect with the Creator and feel what you were intended for.

I ran back out of the woods, along the river again until I came to a small brook, giggling among rocks and then joining its bigger sibling. I went to the edge and stood on flat rocks and leaned over and dipped my hands in the cool water, felt the stones in the earth, felt the eternal flow of the brook becoming part of something else. Leaves passed by, and I wished them well on their journey. I had no intent, only to feel what was there, which became a sacrament of sorts.

Sometime in the decades of exploring I have learned that my closest experiences with God have been in moments like these. Not in complex architecture, not under soaring painted ceilings or among friezes and dour icons, or among marble and carved Latin. I respect those places, and I will always include them in my life. But somehow in nature, where there is less, it is more.

No matter your faith, or where you usually go when you worship, it has probably been disrupted by the way of our world right now. The world and all that is in it, including churches and forests, have in them elements of the Creator. All we need to do is to take the moment needed to see it, and in whatever way is your way, to connect with it. To think, to give thanks, to pray, to ask, to grieve, to find peace.

Hope this finds you finding your way,

David

MURMURATION

January 2012

Greetings from the tips of my wings,

I have this word on a list of things I have been carrying around for a month or so, adding things and scratching things off. I left it in a pocket and couldn't find it for a few days, but it didn't matter. It is under my skin. The word is 'murmuration'.

Last week I saw clouds of starlings, swarming back and forth, creating shapes in the sky. Sweeping across the road out over a field, doubling back and forming dark waves, then spreading out almost invisible in the gray sky, then reforming in dark living pools over me.

You've seen this phenomenon, I hope, somewhere in the sky around you. It is one of those events for which the word 'awesome' was originally created, before surfers kidnapped it and made it as common as Kleenex. When you see it for the first time you are amazed and perhaps frightened and then … inspired.

Ornithologists might explain this swarming in dry bird words, but I like to think the starlings do it for a far more poetic reason. You think so too because when you see it, you want to join them.

A flock of starlings is a murmuration, a word I love rolling around in my mouth. Makes me smile to have a word so unusual to describe something so awesome.

I think that starlings swarm and swirl and make shapes in the sky because it's what they do when they have a reason to celebrate. Like when you hear Sly & The Family Stone play "Thank You Falettinme Be Mice Elf" and you either dance or explode.

When you are brimming with whatever is inside you and something pushes you over the edge into doing what you absolutely must do, must express, must say because it is the natural outlet of who you are, possibly who you are when you are at your best.

I have a list in one of my pockets that starts with "What I am doing when I'm at my best." It is something I have circled back to again and again, and as the year closed, I started the list once more. One of the things on that list is "Celebrating."

A few of you might be tempted to roll your eyes here. Might seem a little superficial to you at first glance. But any of us probably feel at our best when we are celebrating. Having a reason to celebrate and doing something about it. Not just making a cake or decorating with balloons, or putting on party hats and throwing confetti, although I'm in favor of any activity that involves cake. Celebrating in the traditional sense is just one part. There is more waiting to be discovered.

When we are children and everything is awesome, we are inspired to celebrate more often. That wears off; it's not sustainable as adults. Life is hard. There are taxes to pay and stains to wash and people to correct. We have serious responsibilities, and it is frivolous to bounce all over creation like life is one big birthday party. Right?

Every one of us is given gifts and the tools to use them in some way. We are put here for reasons we don't always understand, but I think we come closest to knowing when we find ourselves where we are at our best.

So, when do you feel you are at your best; when you are complaining about how hard things are, or when you celebrate a moment that elevates your heart rate, and your smile can barely keep from turning into laughter? So pretend you get to choose: how do you want to spend your day today?

Perhaps not every moment inspires celebration, but the further apart those moments are, the more your life can feel like someone else's to-do list. And we choose, no matter what our day is like, what we celebrate.

The other great lesson from the starlings is that when we celebrate, and really express it, the joy becomes contagious; it is fluid and natural and overwhelming and soon you find others around you pick up on it, and swarm and swirl with you. That's one of the moments when I feel I am at my best.

So here is what it is: first, I am challenged to really look at what I do in each day, and then push myself into places where I am doing what is the best expression of my gifts and my passions. To live where I am at my best.

And on that list is to Celebrate. To find the moments that are valuable and important, those that I decided, not the calendar, not Hallmark, and hold them up and laugh or sing or eat a piece of cake, find a way of marking the moment. And share it.

I am looking over the leading edge of this year, thinking of how I would make this calendar better than the last, these days more satisfying, challenging, and fulfilling. I will shape what I do intentionally, not let the days accumulate around me like lint. I will figure out where I am at my best, and be there. It starts with this list.

Among other things on the list of "… at my best" is when I am writing to you each Monday. I want to thank you for that privilege. I hope it gives you as much pleasure as it brings me. Happy New Year.

Hope this finds you swarming,

David

REASONS

August 2020

Greetings from the reasons we make,

Yesterday I was talking with my brother, Doug. I didn't have a reason to call; it was just time, or past time, probably. We ended up laughing, a common exchange no matter the conversation. A few times while talking to him, I laughed so hard a crowd gathered to see what all the noise was about. After I hung up yesterday, I could still feel the pleasure of the laugh. I even laughed remembering how hard we laughed.

It is a welcome feeling, this expression of happiness, a smile that cannot be contained, that must be more. Laughter is a celebration.

My daughter's daughter, Ila, has reminded me of a principle of living a satisfying life; to celebrate. She is so new to life our focus is on every increment that seals her safe passage into this world. And then seeing her eyes follow our hand, and reach for it, and then her first smile, her first food, when she turns over. Wow.

There are few other places where we are so willing to celebrate than with a baby. We are not shy about applauding when she blows a bubble of spit, or poops, or puts her finger in her nose. And of course, she will stand and then take the first steps, and there will be first words, firsts after firsts, all anticipated, and then joyfully celebrated.

But we are self-conscious about second steps, and third, until steps are mundane and ordinary. We would not call all our relatives to tell them that our twenty-six-year-old son just took a step.

Birthdays and anniversaries and other milestones are easy places for us to start. Achievements at the end of real effort, or momentous occasions like weddings or graduations. Of course, we should applaud these moments and share the joy in them.

But I suggest looking for other reasons to celebrate. My twenty-six-year-old son took a step, one of many, that will lead to satisfying work, meaningful relationships or achievements or simply building a rich, fulfilling life. Somebody get candles for the cake.

You might think that constant celebration would diminish its impact, that it would feel unnatural and inauthentic. You might wonder whether, if we celebrate everything that happens it will diminish real, significant reasons to acknowledge. I say, take that chance.

I hesitated to write this but here I am anyway; celebrate what you take for granted. Not long ago my son Sawyer was hit by a car. It was a terrifying thing, and thankfully it was no worse than it was. When it was time to leave the emergency room, and he swung his legs off the bed and stood, took his first step, it was a moment of such joy and relief, such happiness, that it deserved celebration. Maybe not appropriate at three o'clock in the morning at Detroit Receiving Hospital, but I would have put candles on the cake and had a party.

You don't have to look for tragedy or near misses, you simply need to acknowledge the gifts we are given and celebrate them. You are a creative and intelligent bunch; you will find the reasons and the ways. I urge you to do it.

At the heart of celebration is the core of happiness: it is being grateful. We could do worse than spending our waking moments seeking reasons to celebrate. We already know that what we focus on in our life will expand, and it's true with this act. Look for reasons to celebrate and they will line up to be counted.

Nature celebrates. Each flower that blooms, every new fawn that bounds, each rebirth of seasons, we see the elements shout, "Waa Hoo!" The light shapes every tree, every stalk of wheat, even the sensual mounds of snow, revealing beauty that was created for us to see. Even as I write this the sun is buttering the grass in gold, calling to me to see how life continues to celebrate.

This is not the first time I've written about this, so I know these things, but knowing and doing can be lifetimes apart. Twelve years ago, I wrote these words: "So, when do you feel you are at your best; when you are complaining about how hard things are, or when you celebrate a moment that elevates your heart rate, and your smile can barely keep from turning into laughter? So pretend you get to choose: how do you want to spend your day today?" I am reminding myself here.

Sips of coffee. Morning light. Birds. The feel of grass on bare feet. An open field. Woods in every season. Words that move us or inspire us when threaded together. Thoughts while running. Seeing, tasting, smelling, feeling, hearing. Sore muscles. The sense of wonder. When we celebrate these things, we are showing gratitude for these gifts. Celebration is prayer.

Our Creator wrote the music before we were born, scribbled a score on some infinite scroll, and set it free into our existence. When we laugh, we express the composition written for us. It is a celebration of the moment, put to music. I believe it is why we are. I love why we are.

Laughter is a celebration of life. You have passion in your life, which I hope you express, and in that act, like laughter, you live out what was given to you, and that in itself is a reason to celebrate. Don't wait for a date, an accumulation of years, or a first step, or the end of a life. Celebrate now.

Hope this finds you choosing joy,

David

HE TANGATA

October 2021

Greetings from the pilgrimage,

> He aha te mea nui o te ao
> He tangata, he tangata, he tangata

Recently I have had the occasion to tell a group of friends that we were in the last miles of a journey. It was not goodbye, just a glance up at the horizon to acknowledge that our paths would diverge. It inspired a familiar feeling, one that I have never resolved in times past, and, spoiler alert, I still have not.

This feeling is like something just out of my peripheral vision, or a word I'm trying to remember. I have a question that seems to want an answer, and the answer is ephemeral, flickering in and out of my thoughts.

Decades ago, I traveled around the country on my bicycle, thousands of miles at a time, and when I sensed that the journey was drawing to a close, I needed to prepare myself for the change, for the transition into the other life. I would ask myself, "What can you bring with you from the road so you will feel the spirit and power of the experience in daily life?"

I thought about this for weeks, months, and I wrote out lessons I thought were important. Some stayed with me, some were sanded off by the ordinary routine of days. But even those lessons were not complete.

I wanted to feel the power of that time on the road, where nothing is separating you and nature. Where there is nothing separating you from your life and living your life. To feel the beauty of creation, and the essence of my own life.

Waking in my hammock, surrounded by the Tetons. Making a small meal by the edge of the Pacific. Grinding up the side of the Rocky Mountains. Standing in the dark in the middle of the Little Mojave, surrounded by a horizon of stars. These images, the mountains, rivers, beautiful sunrises, clouds of starlings, crashing surf, snow squalls, storms of locusts, and countless miles of pedaling over the earth, these are part of what I am now, and part of the lessons, but not the answer.

A few months ago, I climbed up Half Dome in Yosemite. It was a literal mountaintop experience, and I felt the echoes of my other adventures in me as we hiked up through the forest, gazed across the edge of the granite at the breathtaking mountains around us. Even as we hiked down, I asked myself the question, "What can you bring with you from this day so you will carry this beauty, feel the spirit and power of the experience in daily life?"

I have been lucky to have run marathons for over thirty years, all over the country. I've enjoyed traveling to the events and seeing new places in this unusual way. Each time is a test, each run a unique exploration of myself, and the chance to be with others who have the same passion for the challenge. We are witnesses for each other.

I finish running the marathon and my mind is filled with experiences, some of them so personal and real that I have never shared them. Some races have pressed me to the edge of my capacity. And even as I catch my breath, even as I stagger toward the shower, I wonder at the magnificence of it, and I ask myself the question, "How will you hold this experience, this terrible beauty, this triumph, this scraping of your very essence? How will you carry this into your daily life?"

I haven't answered this completely, but here's an important part of my thinking. It was given to me by a young woman who documented her 2650-mile hike along the Pacific Coast Trail. As she approached the last weeks of her adventure, hiking with her group of new trail partners into Washington, she sensed the same question all of us feel as we reach the end of a journey. She wanted the experience to matter, to be relevant in her daily life, to be present no matter where her next path took her. And it led her to a Māori parable, which asked:

'He aha te mea nui o te ao
He tangata, he tangata, he tangata.'

What is the most important thing in the world?
It is the people, it is the people, it is the people.

Ah. We are closer to the answer that matters.

When I was on the road, surrounded by the brilliant, beautiful world, it was the people I met that would often create the character of the day. Those that traveled with me, or fed me, or helped me, or those I helped. Many times, I was invited in by strangers and cared for. Those are the stories that shaped me.

The climb of Half Dome was so awe-inspiring I am often at a loss to share it with others, but it was my friends and family, especially the spirit of my sister Leslie, that climbed with me that made the day what it was. It was our little clan, soaking in the Merced River after twelve hours of hiking. Those people and our connection are what I carry with me now.

The twenty-six miles and some of the marathons are filled with hills and vistas and rain and tailwinds and tragedies and victories. Each place I have run has its own personality. There are many lessons I've learned in those challenging events, and it is the people I met in those endless steps that stay with me, most of whose names I never knew.

I stood with my friends last week and we talked about these last miles of our trip together and we touched on our experiences and what we'd accomplished in our history. But what felt most right was when I shared the story that summed up all of the work and the collaboration and the synergy. The real tangible thing that we carried out of that room into our daily lives was friendship. It was the people.

The people are the living lessons. What do you bring from the road, from the mountain, from the run, from the experience where you were closest to your absolute self? How do you carry with you the experiences of your work, your passions, your adventures? I don't know all the answers, but I feel the one that matters most is this: Whatever else influenced you in those important moments, it was the people who brought you the real lessons. And it is the people you share that with in the days ahead.

It is the people you mentored. It is the people who cared for you. It is the people who shared a space big enough for both of you to grow. It is the people who demonstrated compassion or taught you friendship. It is the people who guided you as a parent. It is those you love, and those you only passed on the trail. It is the people you will have coffee with today, and those who wait for us on the other side. It is the people.

This morning a voice gave shape to the answer, so powerful it brought me to tears. It is the people. What is so exciting for me in this is that whatever life brings me next, I know that in those days of beauty and adventure, there will be the people who will be most important. My world will never be diminished, no matter how I fill the hours, as long as I seek them out.

Hope this finds you taking this into your daily life,

David

SOUNDS OF THE HOUSE

January 2008

Greetings from the sound booth,

I love to listen to music, and I like variety, but lately I have had less tolerance for what is on the radio. I still have my favorites from classic rock and roll, but I find myself straining to hear something fresh and original, something with character.

That's why I was paying attention when I heard just a slice of a song from a group named "Grizzly Bear." It was a strange mix of sounds: muted banjo, piano, and subdued percussion, and behind it, ghostly vocals. The sound was old and subtle, mixed with a techno edge.

The feel of the music was different, and when I heard the group interviewed, I found out why. The album, called "Yellow House," was recorded in an old house. The band incorporated what they found there: pots and pans, cupboard doors, an old out-of-tune piano, a rocking chair. The sound of the music held the character from the house where they lived, not a soundproof, controlled studio. The music did more than include the acoustics of the house; it absorbed the feel of the house.

I know little about making music, even less about recording, but I recognize the feeling from the music. I have been thinking about it all this week as I listened to the sounds of my own house.

In winter the wind can roar across the fields next to us and even with the line of trees near our house it makes a howl around the windows, down the chimney. There is the hum of the refrigerator, mindlessly cycling up and down to keep the milk cool. The snick of dog nails on the wood floor, a clink of his collar bling. The furnace whispers warm reassurance.

Water running in the shower upstairs, playing the pipes in the walls, rattling as the water is slammed off, tick tick ticking as the pipes cool. The clock in the hall chimes, just a tad too slow because it needed winding a few days ago. The phone rings.

Sound levels go up and down with the population level. My children make enough noise on their own, but matched with their friends, the racket goes up exponentially. Laughter, arguing, cheering, and the rumble of stampeding feet.

I can tell which son is coming down the stairs by the cadence of footfalls as they descend. I can hear when four teenagers converge on the bathroom at the same time, even when I can't make out the words they are using.

When you open the silverware drawer, it slips in the track just a bit and rattles the forks and spoons, a jangle and clunk. The tea kettle whistles. The back door moans a little when opened. The floors squeak. The phone rings. The storm door rattles when it closes. Someone is coming home; there is the vibration from the garage door opener. There is a Velcro kind of schrrccch when you open the front door. It makes the dog bark.

Homework is being done. Rummaging in unlikely drawers for scissors, paper, pencils. The stereos pump out music for better concentration. The phone rings. The electric pencil sharpener grinds off what's not needed, sounding angry for being disturbed.

Toilets flushing, lunch bags being crushed into backpacks, Cheerios raining into glass bowls, clothes hampers being dragged down the stairs, thumping resentment at each step. The phone rings. Talking, arguing, yelling, laughing, joking, asking, reminding, scolding, disagreeing, apologizing, praying. And pleading: will someone get that phone?

The kids make their own music. Practice, practice, practice. Trumpet, guitar, piano, cello, bass. They sing. There is kitchen dancing, music bumping from the Bose, shuffling on the wood floors while the clean plates get put away, clinking glasses and cups in time.

In this quiet time this morning, there is only the click of the keyboard, the huff of the coffee pot, impatiently reminding me to have another cup. And this other music; it isn't a sound, but it is. I can hear my family here, sleeping, growing, dreaming.

Just as the music from "Yellow House" took on the sounds of the house it was recorded in, I am etched with the sounds of my home. I sound different because of the noises made here. I sound richer, more complete. What better music is there?

Hope this finds you listening,

David

GREEN ROOM

June 2009

Greetings from stage left,

We wait in the Green Room, which is not green. It is a storage area when we are not here. It is a long narrow room with high ceilings. Paneled single-pane windows look out over a small courtyard. The walls are bare brick; they conduct the outside temperature perfectly, adding to the very informal feel of the Green Room.

There is a table littered with pizza boxes and paper napkins. A few chairs line one wall between the windows. Coats and programs and pieces of sound equipment crowd the edges of the room. Tacked to the doorjamb is the show's lineup. There is a sign that says: "Be polite." No one has challenged it.

A little over a year ago, I joined a group putting on a live radio program in front of an audience. It is a bare-bones affair, held on stage in an old opera house in one of the county parks. There is humor, some tongue-in-cheek drama, and a little culture, but the seats are usually filled with people who come to hear the music.

I stand leaning against the wall, reading my script and thinking about what might have been funnier. My part in the program is a forgettable few minutes of fill between the real talent, but everything is what you make of it. I scribble changes in the margins, trying to make more of it.

The program always features musicians, regional players who crisscross the Midwest. The kind of artists who have day jobs. They play at art fairs and coffee shops, house concerts and anywhere else they can get in front of a crowd.

Through the doorway, the sound of the audience clapping and laughing, urged on by the MC on stage. The cast moves in and out of the room, pacing the hall leading to the stage, quietly chatting about other things so they can avoid being nervous about the show. They tiptoe on the hardwood floors leading to the stage and listen for the tone of the audience during the warmup.

In the relative quiet of the Green Room, the musicians huddle together along one wall. Rod and Jason are tuning their guitars, swapping stories about how long they can keep a pick. Rod says he has had this one for ten years. We all look skeptically at him.

Annie sits on a folding chair, a banjo resting on her knees. Behind her are a couple of guitars and a mandolin. In a small circle next to her are three singers; they are leaning in, serious musicians, intent on what she is saying.

She is leading them through the song. They will be singing together on stage soon and they are looking for harmony in the last few lines. Annie plays up and down the banjo for a minute and then leads them into the chorus:

"Heaven and I, it's a lovely by and by, take this heartache to the sky, leave me there just heaven and I."

The lyrics are lighthearted and whimsical, but I am not really paying close attention to what they mean. There is something else.

The four musicians had just met. Three chorale singers, dressed neatly and formally, sitting knee to knee with Annie in her folk singer ensemble, her knee-high moccasins. Some combination of science and talent and magic, and in a few moments, they produce a beauty that makes the hair on my arms stand up.

The two men behind them are lightly tuning up but seem to be part of the music too. They weave in and out of the banjo sound with their guitars, almost unconsciously chiming into the musical conversation of the other four.

I forgot about what I was doing, and for a moment forgot that the show was going on twenty steps away. A few hundred people sat in the audience waiting for the stage to fill, not knowing that the real show was playing in the narrow storage room next to the stairs.

I looked around at the others in the room, and knew they were witnesses too. Somebody's son, waiting for his mom to come off stage. The foley artist, taking a quick break. The stage manager, clipboard clenched in one hand, typically nervous about when the next act goes up, leaned against the brick and watched the musicians change the room.

Later, on stage, I heard them sing the song, leading the audience through the chorus so they could sing along if they wished. It was nicely done, and the crowd applauded enthusiastically. But there was something different about the sound of the song I heard in the Green Room. It was something intimate and pure and extraordinary.

It is a gift for those who anxiously fidget, waiting to walk the tightrope in front of the audience. This bit of camaraderie that comes with the cold pizza and warm root beer. And to bless it all, a slice of music conjured up by four new friends who share a special talent, this timeless, universal language.

Hope This Finds You

I am not a musician, but I think I saw a glimpse of what brings people to that discipline. Through the practice and the expense and the false starts and the search for the right instrument. Beyond the questions that keep people from trying unicycles and banjos because they are impractical. Out where passion rules.

Hope this finds you in tune,

David

CHRISTMAS CARD

December 2013

Greetings from the greeting,

The room was technically a rectangle, but it had been so long since anyone had seen the original shape that it was unlikely a visitor would be able to testify to that fact. The walls were crowded with tables, old desks, and piles of papers, magazines, and old drawings. The open space where the two men worked was an approximate triangle carved in the flotsam.

Two desk lamps lit the center of the room, green glass shades over mismatched bulbs, spilling two ovals of yellow-white light on the desktops. Dust motes floated aimlessly into the light. Plates with scraps of lunch, from today and other lunches, crowded the workspace. The two men sat facing each other, or would have been if they had looked up. Both held their heads in their hands as if they shared the same migraine.

They had worked across the desk from each other for almost fifty years. They had both joined the company when LBJ was president, started as apprentices, worked for peanuts, held on until someone saw what they could do. They were partners from the first words they wrote on paper. Hank and Chet.

Hank and Chet. It was a brand now; all their cards had the names embossed on the back, along with the prices in U.S. and Canadian currency. Hank and Chet. They didn't even use their last names on the paychecks anymore.

Five decades of writing greeting cards. Funny, inspirational, silly, serious. Holidays, birthdays, occasions or no occasions. Belated thank you, humorous graduation, romantic New Year, condolences for the loss of a pet, congratulations on legalization of same-sex marriage. They filled in the blanks for tongue-tied teenagers and husbands who forgot how to say, and grateful parents and proud stepmothers, absent friends.

They wrote like it was the most natural thing they could do, and it always seemed to work out. They had been stuck before, and one or the other would break the logjam and the ideas would roll out and they would scribble and draw until they left exhausted. And they would produce cards. Good ones.

But not now. They had been staring at blank paper for a solid week, both of them filling whole wastebaskets with ideas; some were bad, and the rest were worse.

"Lissen lissen . . ." Chet said, snapping his fingers to get his partner to look up, "this is it: 'Making Holiday Memories are like lighting candles, . . . they make the moments brighter.' Close up of a candle, real kinda frosted lens shot."

"It's too cliché," sighed Hank.

"Really? You're worried about cliché? You just threw away your best offer: 'Hope you're squeezin throughout the season.' Jee-Zuss. I'm gagging."

"The couple hugging on the cover was the key," said Hank, clasping his own shoulders to demonstrate an embrace.

Chet said nothing. He pinched his nose, like he smelled something sour.

Hank scribbled a drawing in front of him: "How about on the cover we have, like, a serious-looking pig, and inside, 'We wish you a very muddy Christmas.'"

"I don't get it."

"Seriously? Come on, you get it, don't be obtuse."

"Pigs and Christmas. Really? I don't get PIGS. Not at Christmas." Chet scowled, his eyebrows dueling under a new layer of wrinkles.

"Then you come up with something."

"Psssh." Chet flipped his hands out in dismissal. "I can't work with you."

The clock on the wall was given to them by the department director, long since passed away, when they won the "LOUIE" award in 1987. There was a small brass plate on the base of the clock. A testimony to brevity, driven largely by their boss's indifference and the engraver's charge per letter, it said: "To Hank & Bob. Congts.'" After that, Hank called Chet "Bob" and it was funny for about ten years, and then not so much.

The clock snicked quietly, pushed the arms around the face until it said nine fifteen. They had been sitting at the desk for twelve hours.

"Here," said Hank. "The cover says, 'You might want to reconsider your naughty . . .'"

"This is a stick figure!" Chet snapped. "This is what we get? I could get my four-year-old grandson to…"

"It's Santa. Here, I'll add a beard." Hank reached for the page. Chet snatched it up.

"Don't bother, it's ridiculous. Let's go back to the nativity theme."

"No, it's over-done. No one is going to reach for another red-flocked card with a star on it. We gotta update. I tole you." Hank raised his hands over his head.

"And I'm telling you; we are not going to put the word 'twerking' in a Christmas card." He wadded the page up angrily and threw it across the desks.

"Fah la. La. La. La. Whatever." Hank folded his arms and lowered his chin to sulk.

The radiators clunked, moaning uselessly behind the piles of paper near the wall. The room was usually too warm, even with the mounds of cardboard insulation between the hot water heater and where the men sat. The room aged: an oval inside a triangle inside a rectangle. Outside the windows, snow began to cover the sills.

Chet sagged in his chair. "Seriously Hank, I am not enjoying this. I gotta get out of this business. It's sucking the life out of me. I can't even enjoy the holidays anymore."

"Again with this," Hank said, throwing his hands up. "What are you going to do? Start over? 'Welcome to Walmart?' That's not a career for us, Chet."

"US? Who asked you?" Chet sputtered, "Stay here, on another Christmas Eve, working on some card nobody is going to remember in a week."

The two men sat staring at one another. Fifty years of creative juices, deadlines, dead ends, arguments and sweating out inspirational messages for people who would never think twice about throwing their work into the trash. And for fifty years they did it anyway. Across the desk, thinning hair, shoulders sloped, thin arms jutting from rolled-up sleeves, crepey skin stretched over brittle bones, Hank and Chet, slightly mismatched bookends, waited each other out.

"You gotta stick it out with me Bob," Hank said finally.

Chet snorted a little and held back a smile. He lowered his gaze to the desk and folded his gnarled hands together as if he were praying for something to change.

The room was quiet, only the sound of Chet's breathing, a little whistling sound from his nose. Hank waited. Chet did not look up. Hank pulled a sheet of paper in front of him, sketched out something freehand, and etched a caption under it. He slid it at Chet.

"Read it."

Chet spun the paper around. A simple line drawing of a box with a single bow.

"Read it out loud. Like you're at the drugstore picking it for somebody," said Hank.

Chet pushed his glasses up so he could rub his eyes and then focused on the paper.

"Your friendship has been the most important gift I've known. I enjoy opening it every day. Merry Christmas."

The page drifted from his hand and settled in front of him. The two men looked at each other across the chaotic desks and felt the years melt away, felt the aches fade and the worries dwindle. The room closed around them, and the piles of paper disappeared, their world shrunk down to a spill of oval light on the stained oak in front of them. They exchanged smiles and said nothing.

Hope this finds you gifted,

David

MEMORY DAY

May 2022

Greetings from the cenotaphs,

Mom gets the little box out of the top drawer, the drawer we never are supposed to look in but me and Elliot look in there when she is at work, and Mrs. Guerra is watching us, but mostly she watches her stories. So we look in there.

Elliot is only three and I am five so I remember better. When we went to the summertarry last year Mom had to push Elliot in the folding stroller, and it took forever because the one wheel is broken and Mom can't get a new one because of the goddam government.

I know it's Memory Day because everyone has American flags on their stoops and Mom gets off early at the Kwik Trip and goes in the other room where the top drawer is.

She told me yesterday there was going to be a parade and we had to wash good in the tub, and not just fart around. And she laid out the clothes for us and used the iron, which she hates and never uses because it makes the lights go out in the kitchen.

And Elliot hates being in the tub, but I used the scrub rag on him and we horsed around a little, until Mrs. Guerra told us to knock it off before she came in there and gave us what for, and so we knocked it off. The water was cold anyway, and it was kind of dirty.

We were supposed to be getting our pajamas on and instead we tiptoed into the other room, but Elliot doesn't tiptoe very good. It didn't matter because Mrs. Guerra had the TV turned up so loud. Mom says she's deffasapost.

So we stood on a basket and we slid open the top drawer and looked in there. There's envelopes that look boring and some coins in a dish and some chocolate and a pack of cigarettes with one already smoked a little and stuck in the plastic wrapper.

And the little box. I take it out and we sit on the floor and open it up and I tell Elliot not to touch it but he always does. It's purple and he likes the color, and he touches the ribbon part, and the little metal heart is purple too, and it has an old-fashioned man's face on it.

I tell him it's Dad's and he doesn't understand, and he thinks that the old-fashioned man is Dad, because he doesn't know what Dad looked like. We put the little box back in the top drawer.

In the morning we didn't get up the first time Mom called us and so she was mad and so Elliott cried a little bit. We had Rice Krispies and because it was Memory Day we got Pop-Tarts. Except at Kwik Trip they are "Toasterlicious." It was a variety pack and Elliot got chocolate and I got cinnamon.

They taste like biscuits Mrs. Guerra makes and they were so dry I had to pick some of it off the roof of my mouth with my spoon. Elliot was grossed out but he laughed so hard that he sprayed milk and Rice Krispies on the table and Mom told us to cut the crap, and Elliot cried a little.

Mom says if we are good we can go to the parade and I wipe Elliot's face and tell her we are going to be super good. I am so excited I can feel bumblebees zooming around in my tummy. We brush our teeth and don't horse around and don't hardly get toothpaste on our ironed shirts.

If we go to the parade there will be fire trucks and clowns that throw candy. Elliot hates the loud fire trucks and clowns scare him, but all I tell him is there will be candy. He forgot the other stuff from last year's Memory Day parade.

Elliot doesn't have hardly any memory because he's only three. I have memory but I have to practice all the time, or some things go away. Like Dad. I have to practice Dad.

Mom tells us to sit in the davenport and we run in there and we both jump on the cushions and make dust float in the sunbeams. I want to be good, but mostly I want to go to the parade, but we have to remember and we have to go to the summertarry. Mrs. Guerra brought flowers for Mom to take and when she saw them her eyes watered and she said she wasn't crying it was because she had goddam hay fever from the flowers.

Me and Elliot sit on the davenport and I put my arm around his neck and tell him to be good and stop kicking his feet. He wants to go to the parade and get candy but I tell him we have to remember and then we can go. He says he doesn't want to remember and he cries a little. And then we wait, and we are super good.

Mom gets the little box out of the top drawer.

Hope this finds you remembering,

David

David Scott Smith

HER GIFT

January 2011

Greetings from a long shadow,

It was the kind of funeral where they had to bring out extra chairs. The pews were full, the choir loft was full, and some folks stood at the back of the church. I know that in slightly different circumstances, we would have been content to sit there all afternoon and listen to stories about Karen, nodding our heads when we heard about something we all had in common through this woman whom we will miss so much.

This will sound self-centered, but I have never been to a funeral where I haven't wondered what people might say about me after I'm gone. Usually, I feel like I should step things up a bit, provide a more interesting eulogy than I have so far.

That was true this time too. Karen was loved and admired; the church was filled with people who could have spent the afternoon and into the night describing what an astounding woman she was.

146

Her life was an extraordinary light for us.

Karen was a friend of mine. I feel a little presumptuous saying that because we knew each other in such a narrow context. But it is true anyway.

We served on a team for over three years, worked in church leadership for a couple more. Lots of long meetings, some long car rides, many long conversations on complicated subjects. In a short time, I realized the caliber of person I was dealing with and to be honest, felt like I needed to step things up a bit.

At first, it was a little intimidating. But there was nothing arrogant or pretentious about Karen. She had style, but she didn't have to tell you she did. She was smart but she didn't have to prove it to you. You simply experienced it, along with her humor, her kindness, her patience, and generosity.

Karen brought a certain class, a grace to the things she put her hand to. She was an elegant host, an inspiring conversationalist, and a deep thinker. She was well-read. She read things that would not occur to me, but she did not spoon-feed anything.

Her son Peter talked about how Karen always put others first and never wanted attention focused on her, "to the point it was almost pathological," he said. She had a gentle way of turning any question about her into a conversation about you.

At the end of the memorial service, Pastor Kristi asked: "What gift did Karen give you? And what are you going to do with it?"

I had time to think about that question. There was a time early yesterday morning in that gray place between not sleeping and not willing to commit to awake. I talked with Karen for a long time to see if I really knew what gifts she gave me. She would say that she did not give anyone a gift as much as awaken the gifts they already had.

One of my favorite things she said was something she repeated several times to people who would ask how she was doing: "I don't want to become a cancer patient. I don't want this to define me." And it didn't.

So, she was never a victim. It seemed to me it was not a matter of arrogance; it simply wasn't what she would choose. That's a lesson I hope I never have to apply, but I have to admit I am inspired by her courage and her integrity.

She was not cavalier about her treatment, but neither did it become who she was. She made plans for her life, taught classes, started ambitious books, and thought about big things. That was who she was before someone named the disease that would end her life. And the naming did not change her.

I think Karen was a true leader. It showed in her demeanor, her thoughtful consideration of important issues, and the way she invited others to be at their best. That might be another gift. This might become quite a list.

So, we come to the second part of the pastor's question, the part that frightens me; what to do with it?

Some of that is already happening; some is still waiting to be revealed, I guess. But one clear thing is the example of living that Karen etched out for us to follow if we are brave enough.

Karen was a woman of faith, of soundly forged principles, of great compassion and generosity, of deep emotion and insight. She was many things to those who cared for her: friend and wife and mother and teacher and mentor. In the space where she was in our lives, we can best honor her memory by carrying forward her gifts. I'm in.

Hope this finds you using what you're given,

David

BOSTON BOMB

April 2013

Greetings from the bubble,

My friend Kirk asked me: "Do you think they will run it again?"

I might have answered with a little more emotion than I intended. I was still in the space between wishing I had been in Boston and relieved I was not. My eyes burned; my chest was tight with anger.

"They won't cancel the Boston marathon. They won't give up. It's 117 years of running. Never."

In Hopkinton, there is a huge open space behind the high school. It is the Athlete's Village for the Boston Marathon. In the hours before the race, it fills up with men and women from around the world, in all manner of physiques, different shades and gaits. But there is a look they have in common. It is passion. It is determination. It is a force of will, the human spirit.

It is a unique environment, something pure and simple. There are no politics or race or economic pecking order. There are competitors, but there is an implicit understanding and respect. Runners sign each other's race bibs, pose for pictures, sit around games of cards or simple pre-race meals. We make idle chatter and wait. We hold hands and pray. A space forms around us. And then we run.

I wasn't with them this year, but I felt their nervousness, felt the jitters, the anxious tension waiting for the gun to go off, to release us onto the downhill, to push back the rest of the world for a few hours and let us run just to run. To demonstrate who we are, to test ourselves in community with others of our kind. In that time, when humanity lines the road to cheer the human spirit, there is a space created, a buffer between the usual and the expected, and this space is filled with an incredible positive energy. It is excitement and joy and triumph and even with the challenge and struggle, it is hope. It is a bubble of sorts. It sometimes seems a fragile thing, this bubble, but it is remarkably resilient.

In 1972 at the Olympics in Munich, the bubble was pierced. Terrorists shredded the thin element that surrounded the games, showed the world that there is nothing sacred or beyond the reach of evil. They used the Olympic stage and stepped into the space formed by the athletes and those who stood to cheer the competitors. They violated the space.

Bill Bowerman, who became one of the founders of Nike, was the track coach who marshaled the athletes. He knew they were afraid, defeated even, before competing. He knew the space that surrounded them had deflated, leaving them stained and confused, doubting the value of the competition.

"If there is one place where war doesn't belong, it is here," Bowerman told them. "For twelve hundred years, Olympians laid down their arms to take part in these Games. They knew there is more honor in outrunning a man than killing him. So, you must not believe that running, or jumping or throwing are meaningless. They were your fellow Olympians' answer to war. They must be yours."

The tragedy unfolded and it seemed the competition was over. But when the Olympic committee determined to let the events restart, the bubble had been pierced. The separateness, the safety, the faint illusion that the games protected them from the world, had leaked out. The athletes huddled together, tense, afraid that there would be more violence. The marathoners debated the sensibility, knowing they could be targets. But in the end, the will to compete, the passion to hold the fire higher so the world could witness, won out.

Frank Shorter, who went on to win the marathon, said: "This is as scared as I'm going to get. Let's run."

Five months ago, the bubble took on a different shape. When Superstorm Sandy devastated the east coast and turned the Big Apple into a dark scary place, 40,000 runners surged toward New York to run the marathon, an overwhelming force. Their message was that the race must go on, the space must be honored.

But the people living in darkness, without water or safety, bristled. Soon the race was seen as frivolous, trivial, irrelevant. The voices said: "Who do these people think they are? Coming here like they are something special? Taking resources from us."

The bubble was an intruder. I didn't think so at first, but of course it was right to cancel the race. The space that is created around the marathon, and events like it, is meant to include, not exclude. The runners who had already arrived, from all over the globe, stayed to help. They cleaned and carried water and made themselves useful. And promised to run again. And in that first moment, the space began to form once more.

In Boston, terrorists used the stage again. But we will not let them take the space we created. After the explosion, people ran from the spot; but look to see who the first responders were. Runners. Men and women who had just completed 26.2 miles of challenge, turned and ran back to the chaos to help. Marathoners literally lined up to give blood. Runners in tears, terrified, held on to one another, and to the people around them, and slowly built strength, renewed resolve. And before the day was over, the space began to build again.

George Sheehan, the runner philosopher, said this: "Winning and losing is what you do in team games. The runner is not in a game; he is in a contest. And that is a word whose Latin root means to witness or testify. The other runners are witnesses to what he is doing. And therefore, anything else than all he can give is not enough. When you race, you are under oath. When you race, you are testifying as to who you are."

We run to testify, and to push those around us, running with us, standing watching us, to do the same. To say: we commit to being the best we can be for ourselves and for each other.

We run to test ourselves. To improve. To inspire. To remember. To represent. To compete. We run not to be separate from the world but to bring the world with us. To testify. To give witness that even in this simple act, we can be as one people. We can rise above the gray dimness that threatens humanity and hold the light high, for ourselves and for those who would run with us.

There is not enough world to hold us back. Not enough violence or disdain or hate or ridicule or fear or cynicism or doubt. We will run again, not because we are elite or different or special, but because we are meant to run, as humans, as companions. We are meant to express ourselves in this way. I believe it.

In Hopkinton, 26.2 miles from Boston, behind the blue and gold starting line with its iconic unicorn, we wait. There is a moment before the big gun goes off, when the anticipation is palpable, and you can feel tens of thousands of people lean forward, eager for the first step. And you look into the eyes of the runner next to you, and you see the miles and the pain and the time and the tears and the failure and the challenge and beginning again and failing and never ever giving up.

It is the human condition, the spirit that keeps us from giving in to what would make us less than what we are meant for. And then we take the first step and run with all we have into the space the world has made.

We will run again.

Hope this finds you testifying,

David

Hope this finds you delighted

"Laughter is carbonated holiness.

~ Anne Lamott

CHRISTMAS TREE

December 2004

Greetings from a man named Bunyan,

I've always wanted to be a lumberjack. I like the idea of being outdoors, wearing big boots and plaid shirts, singing that special Lumberjack Song, and swinging a big sharp tool.

That's why I always look forward to tramping out into the woods with my family and capturing a Christmas tree, right out of the ground. Armed with only my lumberjack instincts and a saw-thing with extra pointy teeth, I like to pit my abilities against the wily pine. Sure, we could buy one at the grocery store from one of those tree gypsies, but then we wouldn't get to wear our big boots and plaid shirt.

Because of a flaw in our planning (namely, we didn't do any), we arrived at the tree farm very close to closing time. If you want the tree farmer to bring you back out of the woods on the hayride, you don't want to keep him out past suppertime. We scurried off into the woods, promising to capture our tree post haste. Generally, lumberjacks do not "scurry."

Ordinarily, when you pick out the tree, you can't take the first one you like. You must look at every other tree in the forest, including the birch trees, and rule them out as too tall, too short, too full, too skimpy in the back, too "struck-by-lightning," etc. Once these are all eliminated, then you may choose the first tree you liked.

By necessity, we selected our tree in under 10 minutes. While this took a little of the magic out of the moment, it appealed to my respect for economy of effort. Whenever you need a euphemism for "lazy," you may use this phrase: "It appealed to my respect for economy of effort." Don't use it in front of lumberjacks, however, or they will pull your suspenders up so high you will see stars.

We loaded our tree, the best one we ever got, and headed back to civilization. Like many intelligent people, I always worry that the tree will blow off the top of the van while I'm driving. I've found that it helps to drive about fifteen miles per hour and hunch your shoulders and clench the steering wheel. Also, whenever you hit a bump or a big truck passes you, you should hold your breath and grit your teeth. This way, the tree will stay tied on with the 200 ft. of yellow nylon rope you tied in 92 granny knots, which will be frozen solid to the van.

Assuming your tree does not stage an escape on the way home, you may now put it in the special Christmas tree stand you bought that is guaranteed not to tip over. In order to get the tree into the tree stand, you must cut off some of the trunk. This galls me because I paid for an eight-foot tree and now I am intentionally cutting off about $20 worth and throwing it back into the woods. If this weren't a Christian holiday, I would say that it was Karma.

Bringing an eight-foot tree into the house is easier than it sounds. Since eight feet is taller than most doors, it helps if you carry the tree in horizontally. (YOU are not horizontal; the TREE is horizontal.)

Once the tree is mounted in the stand and put into the correct place in your home, you are required by the Michigan Department of Illuminated Trees to make sure that the tree is perfectly vertical. I have a certified representative of the Michigan Department of Illuminated Trees residing in our home, who guided me in the tree verticalizing. It was a complicated and painful process. This is how I discovered our house was crooked. Having a crooked house explains why I can never get a picture to hang level or make a good omelet.

After pushing the tree, pulling it, adjusting it, cutting the trunk, and shaving half an inch off the carpet, I was finally able to get the tree to appear straight. However, now all the furniture looks like it's leaning.

One thing I learned this year is that I don't know how to put lights on the tree. Somehow, I missed the light-stringing class in high school. I understand it is part science, part art, so maybe it was one of those "elective" classes like marching bandsaws or musical chair-drafting. Or Bio-sketching. Or Chemistry-Interpretive Dance. (Went too far, didn't I?)

I made the effort, even struggling with the ignorance, to get the lights on the tree, but Suzanne gave me several stern warnings before I was directed to put down the lights and step away from the tree. Once I was safely horizontal on the couch, I could see the glaring problems of poorly distributed tree lights. I have to hand it to my wife; she is far better at hanging those lights than I am. As much as it pains me to say it, next year I may have to lay on the couch again while she puts those lights on the correct way.

Thursday afternoon, the kids decorated the tree. This year they were actually able to get the ornaments on the tree with only a moderate risk of injury. There is quite a menagerie of decorations; glass bulbs from when I was a boy, paper bells from some kindergarten project, crystal, plastic, tin and string, all adding some color, texture and history to our best tree we ever got. And every year we hang that one ornament made with a picture of some kid we can't identify. If it's one of you, please write back.

The best part about the Christmas tree process is basking in the glow of the carefully arranged light strands, thinking about that special night that will be here before we know it, and yet is taking forever to get here.

Hope this finds you feeling sappy,

David

DISHWASHER

September 2003

Greetings from behind the chaos,

There are six people who live here, plus the hundred or so children who visit each day. We generate a lot of dirty dishes, as you can imagine, and since we are a civilized group, we make attempts to wash the dishes before we use them again. Clean dishes are a mark of an advanced society, rarely seen in primitive cultures where they rely solely on takeout food.

When I was a single person, I didn't have a dishwasher; I washed my dishes in the sink. There were only a couple of things to wash since I usually ate over the sink anyway. Silverware could be cleaned immediately after use by wiping vigorously against my blue jeans. Whenever I was entertaining, I would soak the dishes in a solution of 1 tsp. vinegar, 1 tsp. ammonia, and one gallon of water, and then serve corn dogs on a stick, which were consumed standing at the sink filled with the aforementioned solution.

Nowadays we have a dishwasher, a really good one with a lot of fancy features. The dishwasher is designed to wash dishes but really has become an extension of the cupboard, by which I mean that there are almost always dishes stored there. The reason is that no one knows if the dishes in the dishwasher are clean or not, and if you open the door to look, someone might ask you to put the dishes away. A regular question in our kitchen is, "Are these clean?"

I know some people who hang a little sign on their dishwasher that has "Clean" and "Dirty" on either side. Then all they have to do is remember to turn the sign over at the right time, and later to believe they remembered to do it. Our fancy dishwasher has a little readout that says the dishes are clean until you open the door and sneak out a glass, leaving the rest of the dishes in dishwasher limbo. The rest of the dishes will be put away "later," a time that has been more accurately described in the book of Revelation.

So the counter near the dishwasher becomes a sort of staging area for the dishes waiting to be washed. When that area is full, then dishes go into the sink, then on to the rest of the counter until we reach the toaster. When we run out of dishes or reach the toaster, it is time to empty the dishwasher. That's when we make ourselves scarce.

You might suggest that we consider paper plates to reduce the number of dishes. (Maybe you weren't going to, but it helps advance my theme, and after all, who is running this show?) Yes, they are gauche and not environmentally friendly, but when it comes to my convenience, I'm willing to risk the ire of tree-hugging Miss Manners types. If there is such a type and if they have such an ire.

I don't mean the fancy Chinette brand, I'm talking about the "Bonus Family Pack" which you can buy anywhere for 99 cents for 5000 plates. Of course, you can't actually separate 5000 plates; they are usually stuck together 122 at a time. These are so thin that we have accidentally served them as soft-shell tortillas, which wasn't all bad with enough salsa on them. The net result is that we wash fewer dishes, but we all have paper cuts from the plates. Perhaps I have digressed from my original theme.

In the past, I would hesitate to load the dishwasher, because I have been told that there is a right way and a wrong way to do this. There is all manner of pins and racks and pockets and holders in the dishwasher, and each must be used appropriately, or we violate our warranty, and/or the Versailles treaty. After my first orientation, which included a video and hands-on demonstration, I became a little intimidated. There is a manual to follow in case I am unsure of my method. Rather than risk the ire of the manual, and the woman holding the manual, I sometimes choose not to load the dishwasher. Not in a fit of pique, mind you.

But I am a grown man with significant life experience, and, I might add, I'm a little bit of a rebel. I have moved past my fear of manual-holder retribution and have taken to loading the dishwasher pell-mell and willy-nilly. When the trays are filled with dirty dishes, then I put an unmeasured amount of soap in the little tray, close the door, and in my most rebellious manner, I push the "Auto Wash" button.

I have also on occasion, usually when the dishes reach the toaster, emptied the dishwasher. I don't always know where some of the more unusual stuff goes, but I can usually get the glasses and plates put in the correct cupboard. Yes, I know the coffee cups go upside down and the glasses go upside up. No, you don't mix the small forks with the big forks in that little tray because who knows what that would lead to.

Not long ago, and I am purposely vague on the date, I was feeling particularly industrious and not a little rebellious, and decided to empty the dishwasher. I put the plates on the plate shelf and the cups and the glasses in their area, dealt the forks and spoons and knives into the correct slots. It wasn't until I reached the pots and pans that I noticed the hardened scrambled egg. A closer inspection of a few of the forks showed some spaghetti sauce between the tines. Hmm. Perhaps these were not clean dishes after all.

But now I have a dilemma. How can I go back and identify all those dirty dishes I put away? I could go back through every shelf and every drawer and search for signs of food on each dish and fork. Or I could take everything out of each shelf and rewash the whole shebang. Hmmm. What should I do? Even better, what DID I do?

Enough time has passed that my decision is not really important. The important thing is that I am continually advancing as a human being, learning things, trying things, and along the way, helping other people. That's what's really important.

Hope this finds you using the phrase "Fit of pique,"

David

BRADFORD PEAR

February 2005

Greetings from someone looking up,

In our back yard we have several trees, including a Bradford Pear. Any fool can tell it's a Bradford Pear tree, and if any fool could not, then he could ask his wife and she will tell. I would not have named this particular tree a pear tree because there have never been pears on it. It might better be called a Bradford Pear-less tree. If it were named for fruit it does not have, it might as well be called a Bradford Watermelon tree. But this is not my point.

I admire this tree for its foolish optimism. It is recklessly hopeful; unreasonably so. It is the type of tree one would be embarrassed to be around because it is so naïve, so expectant, so willing to believe. For all I know, this tree thinks it can grow pears. Or watermelons.

When fall comes, it eventually changes the color of its leaves, but it will not let them go. Because long after the other trees have resigned themselves to winter's grip, this pear tree holds on to the thought that summer might come back, there might be a sunny spell around the corner, and you don't want to be leafless when that happens.

It is a sad day when the Bradford Pear finally gives up its leaves. The ground is white with snow, a thick winter blanket covering the litter left by less optimistic trees. Around the pear tree is a brown apron of leaves, tiny wet soggy flags of surrender.

The pear tree then assumes the grim naked stance of its deciduous brothers and sisters in the yard. Clacking their limbs in the wind to stay warm, these trees stand stoic in their austere station. They are pretending not to be jealous of the pine trees that are wrapped in a plush coat of green needles, bundled against the winter cold. They are jealous, though. They are green with envy. They want the winter to be over so they can pull on their spring foliage, pin on the flowers, the berries, the little whirlybird accessories that will make them beautiful again.

I want winter to be over too, and yet I know that warm weather is not close at hand. I know there will be other arctic blasts, more snow to shovel, more weeks of bundling the kids in layers to brave the conditions. I know that the sun will be a dim gray semblance of its summer self for months to come.

To add to this frosty slap of reality, Punxsutawney Phil, that Pennsylvania rodent-prognosticator, in a fit of insecurity has predicted six more weeks of winter, which he does 87% of the time. Phil is not an optimist; he lives underground, if that tells you anything about him.

The Bradford Pear does not care what the groundhog has to say. It does not acknowledge the Farmer's Almanac. It has stood in frozen earth long enough. It summons every bit of courage it has in its chlorophyll-starved frame, reaches deep into its roots, and pushes out; its bark is shivering with effort.

Hope This Finds You

This weekend I looked into the yard and saw that the pear tree was sprouting little white buds on the ends of its branches. Tiny little buds, brave pioneer sprouts, ignoring peer pressure from the maples. The Bradford Pear defies nature, dares winter to stay. It calls out for spring to come, to free us from the damp cold days, to banish the puddles deep into the woods where more cowardly trees live.

People tend to see the signs they want to see. Some gather in frozen knots around a clownish rodent, imposter that he is, and wait to be told more grim news. This morning, I stood at the window and found myself cheering for this heroic effort in my backyard. Foolishly optimistic or not, this is the direction I choose.

Hope this finds you budding,

David

BATS IN THE BELFRY

August 2008

Greetings from Quasimodo,

I like nature, but I like to be in control of how much nature comes into my house. It's why we have air conditioning and doorknobs that only certain primates can operate.

We have more than our share of woodland creatures loitering about. Deer, fox, raccoon, possum, mole, and possibly some very well-concealed feral pigs. Other than a few mice, none of these have ventured indoors where we civilized animals reside. Until this week.

I have bats in my belfry. This will not surprise anyone who knows me, having witnessed my helter-skelter pell-mell willy-nilly approach to an average day. But in fact, aside from being heltered and skeltered, I actually have bats in my belfry.

Technically, I don't have a belfry, much to the relief of the neighbors, since I would be ringing the bells at all hours yelling, "Sanctuary! Sanctuary!" The closest thing we have to a belfry is our chimney. I know an entire family who referred to this as a "chimbley." They were so confident in their pronunciation that for a while I thought I was saying it wrong. Whichever it is, that's where the bats are.

The bats have been squeaking and chattering up in their lair for some time. In my skeltered, oblivious state, I had no idea until Suzanne told me.

She motioned me into the bedroom, urgently whispering my name, which I took entirely the wrong way. For the record, I'll admit that I tend to look for the wrong way, so this was entirely my fault.

"I think we have bats in our chimney," she whispered. She said it so low I thought at first she said, "don't hang your hat on our chimbley." Well, of course not.

I listened and, sure enough, heard a quiet chorus of squeaking coming from the chimney.

My first thought was, "Do bats make a squeaking sound?" and then, "I wonder if today I should go to the beach," followed by, "Chocolate Moose Tracks is my favorite."

Suzanne wanted to keep it a secret, like it was some scandal that our family should hide from the neighbors. I agree, and that's why I'm keeping it between you and me.

After a brief one-hour search, I found a flashlight and shone it up into the chimney and, sure enough, there was a group of something that could have been bats roosting in our chimney. Honestly, I don't know bats from shinola, so they could have been feral pigs as far as I was concerned.

It turns out we don't have bats in our belfry; they are birds. I believe they are a rare species called the Chimbley Warbler.

The next part of the strategy was to force the birds out of the chimney. There are probably more scientifically sound methods, but someone suggested starting a fire in the fireplace. This actually worked for a few hours, but the birds came back as soon as we tried going to sleep. I think they were singing louder than before just out of spite.

The next morning one of the birds actually descended through the flue and was fluttering against the glass of the fireplace. After another whispered directive from Suzanne, which I again took the wrong way, I was resigned to capturing the bird. I put on a heavy pair of gloves originally designed for falconry and selected a bird trap device originally designed to contain yogurt.

The actual capture was not as smooth as you might imagine, even if you have a really good imagination. There was a brief struggle, during which I stunned the bird and he fell into the container. I think that's what happened; I was actually looking the other way.

As I walked through the backyard, feeling the bird scuffling inside the yogurt container, all I could think of was the Alfred Hitchcock thriller "The Birds." I imagined that somehow the bird's squeaks were transmitting an S.O.S. to the other birds in the area. Suddenly, I felt like a million beady eyes were watching me, and the hair on my neck stood up. I began to run.

I ran through the backyard, holding the yogurt tub in front of me, part of me determined to get the bird far enough from the house so he wouldn't be tempted to come back, and part of me just wanting to be rid of it before birds started attacking me.

Right at that moment, a pinecone fell from the tree above me and hit me on the top of the head, which is the first time this has ever happened to me so as far as I'm concerned it feels exactly like a Chimney Warbler trying to peck into my Sagittal suture. I think at that point I accidentally made a sound like a feral pig. A girly feral pig.

The birds came back the next day, cheerfully singing in the shower-like acoustics of our belfry. The solution is fairly easy. You put a cap on the chimney, which allows the heat to escape but doesn't allow nature to come in. This requires a trip to the hardware store, and then a little time on the roof with some tools.

So, the first free moment I had, I packed up the kids and went to the beach.

Hope this finds you with a bird in the hand,

David

LEARNING CHESS

October 2017

Greetings from the novice,

I am learning how to play chess. Those words may cause some people to wince, particularly considering my short attention span, impatience, and the fact that I don't like to learn new things or look stupid or lose. Or play chess.

It is widely held that chess was created in the Far East, perhaps in the sixth century, definitely before Netflix. Originally, the players would sit on the same side of the table while playing so they would not be tempted to hurl the chess pieces at each other. This changed in the seventh century because of all the stabbings, when the players had to be separated. I may have made some of this up.

The chessboard in our house held basically the same space as my golf clubs. Gathering dust, months and years piling up and coating all the motivation with a thick layer of inertia. Both chess and golf have remained on the Permanent List of Things I Will Do Someday When I Have Time.

Chess is a lot like golf. In both cases, there is a certain amount of patience required before giving up and throwing things into a pond. I really have no business making this comparison, given that I have less than zero experience in either game/sport. I do know I would not spend a Sunday afternoon watching someone else play either game/sport.

Chess is a lot like checkers. No, it's not. Other than the board looks similar. Some boards can be folded up and used as a rectangle. This is handy when trying to keep dust from accumulating in a rectangular area.

There are 64 squares on the chess board, but I've found that you don't use many of them if your opponent takes your pieces using some complex Kasparovian strategy that works really well against someone with a short attention span. I know the number of squares on the board (64) because I stared at them for so long while trying to remember which way the Pawn can move.

I have not reached the point where I can employ chess strategy, other than to wait until it's my turn to move. I am too tied up learning which way the various pieces can maneuver. It's exhausting. Consider the Knight:

"The Knight shall not move to a square which is adjacent to itself, neither in a straight line nor that of the diagonal. The Knight shall first only move two squares, and the number of squares it shall move first shall be two. Three squares it shall not move, nor as previously described, not one square for that is one too few. Once the Fair Knight hath moved two squares, then only shall it move to the left or to the right, of its own desire, and advance then only one square. If in its journey this Noble One should find others of its party, it may regally leap over them to achieve its quest."

There are sixteen pieces on my side of the board, and in theory I am supposed to know what to do with them to somehow get them in position to vanquish my opponent. So far, all I have been able to do is memorize the names of the pieces: The Pawn, the Clown, the Studebaker, the one with the Pointy Hat, and then the Queen and King. I think that's sixteen.

My first game was fun, I'll have to admit. Fact is, the game is so complex I didn't realize I had lost until I realized my wife had already left the table and was loading the dishwasher. (I thought it was a very involved chess gambit.) I was still sizing up my next foray when she turned off the lights and went to bed, which at the time seemed like a bold move to flank my queen. Since I can't actually be sure which piece is the queen, it could have been in the dishwasher for all I know.

Chess is a lot like a kid's birthday party. It starts out all neat and orderly but then chaos ensues, and someone is going home unhappy. Hmm, still not it.

What I have learned so far is that chess requires thinking. This is an activity I am not intimately acquainted with, but even at my advanced age, I'm probably ripe with potential. It's not like I am unfamiliar with the concept of thinking but, like a lot of things, it's different in application versus reading about it in a comic book. I have also learned you don't say "Checkmate" after each move.

For a short time, I thought I might be a chess prodigy, until I played chess. And then looked up the word "prodigy." This has also cast a shadow of doubt on my dream of being a violin prodigy.

Chess is like a lot of things you could enjoy if you employ these two ideas: enjoy the process instead of focusing on the outcome, don't take it too seriously, and, most important, keep your head down and your eyes on the ball. I think that's more than two, but you get the point.

Hope this finds you castling,

David

WHISTLE PIG

May 2022

Greetings from the top of the food chain,

If you think about it, we have a very strange relationship with animals. If we had to explain it to Martians, it would sound hilarious.

Us: See, these animals we ride, those are for pulling things but not riding, and these animals are for eating. Some animals we keep in cages to look at, and some we keep in cages to eat their young. But these animals over here, we don't eat.

Martians: Why not?

Us: These are pets, we don't eat our pets. We feed them and spend outrageous amounts of money to care for them, and when they poop in public, we pick it up and carry it. Often, we will push them in pet perambulators so they don't have to walk. They are like royalty.

Martians: We are going to take over now.

In my house we are executing ants. Technically, they are not animals, so you may see it as off-topic, but I want to mention this because I hope our reputation gets out and other ants will think twice about walking around on our kitchen counter. Anyway (as my Mom would say when she wanted to change the subject) —animals.

I live at the edge of a forest, which brings me in close contact with animals daily. Lots of birds, a few snakes, a bazillion squirrels, some chipmunks. I have never seen a koala here or a feral shoat, although the woods are lovely, dark and deep, and they easily could hide both.

Sometimes the animals try to come into our house. Birds often crash into the windows, some kind of protest about the quality of food we give them, I think. We have had bats in our belfry and mice will sometimes find shelter in warm nooks and crannies here, where they are not welcome. I have dealt with these invaders in the same way ants are dispatched and with only slightly more regard. Woodpeckers occasionally put holes in the house, which up until now I have forgiven, because they are pretty and too hard to catch. You might sense an uneven scale of justice emerging.

Every day there are deer in the yard. Deer are welcome, except when they eat things we planted not to be eaten, a sort of Edenic irony. These delightful fragrant plants, which are delicious but not to be tasted, we must spray with noxious potions in the futile hope that it will spoil the appetite of the deer. But deer are so pretty and graceful, and they don't attempt to come into the house, so it's hard to be angry at them.

Easier to be angry at are groundhogs, also known as woodchucks (from that rhetorical math poem) and my favorite appellation, "whistle pigs."

We are being harassed by a terrorist whistle pig, which is the first time in history those words were put in that order in a sentence. This wily marmot has been digging caves around the foundation of our house, which is not only unsightly but also sets a bad precedent for other varmints. And it's unsightly. Does anyone ever say something is "sightly"?

We decided to humanely trap the whistle pig and have him/her/them taken gently to some other woods where justice is tilted to allow whistle pigs, whatever their gender preference, to live out their natural span. We hired an expert, who has proven to be cheerfully willing but woefully inept. He put an ear of corn and some cabbage leaves in the trap, which rumor has it is the whistle pig's Happy Meal.

I checked the traps every time I walked past the window, which is too often. Immediately the traps were sprung, and we found we had caught some sticks. Another time a trap was sprung, perhaps by the wily feral koala, and something ate the corn right through the cage. So, I guess we caught cabbage leaves.

Then we caught a raccoon. This might have been kind of a victory, except for the look the raccoon gave me, which seem to say, "Can you believe this? Even a whistle pig doesn't fall for a trick so rudimentary."

Then we caught a possum. Also a false victory, although possums are very unattractive so I was glad he got relocated. I know it's not fair, but I feel like he was bringing down the average of the yard, looks-wise. I think I can be that prejudiced if I begin the sentence with "I know it's not fair..."

It feels like the whistle pig is toying with us, spreading false Happy Meal rumors, daring other varmints to explore the cages, predicting Spring with no basis in meteorology. I'm tempted to give up, but I have promises to keep.

The spectrum of our relationships with animals is erratic and irrational and it's better not to try to explain it to Martians, as if they would bother to ask. They are likely much more curious about WWE, disc golf, and meaningless memes about mean Twitter texts. Anyway. I can't worry about what Martians think when there are so many other fabricated concerns to keep me awake. And miles to go before I sleep.

I just checked the traps for the tenth time this morning, which if you are following along is precisely the number of times I went by the window, and also the precise number of times we have not captured a whistle pig. I am sure if I'm consistently obsessive, eventually we will catch something besides everything else other than a whistle pig, but I have other fish to fry. And miles to go before I sleep.

Hope this finds you stopping by woods,

David

COLONOSCOPIES ARE FUNNY

May 2021

Greetings from a humorous view,

Those of you with sensitive dispositions may wish to avert your eyes while reading this.

A colonoscopy is not funny. But really, it is hilarious. The idea of it still makes me laugh. I don't think having one is funny, but you have to admit the process and the procedure is so ludicrous that, taken out of context, it's hysterical.

To prove the comedy, I would time travel back to the 1800s and explain it to a doctor then.

"I have traveled back in time from 2021 to tell you about an amazing medical procedure."

"Why are you dressed like a tramp? Has there been a terrible war?"

"No, this is just how I look."

"I see. Don't people dress to travel in your era? All right, tell me your amazing news."

"Well, in the future, medical doctors will put cameras inside you to see if you are healthy."

Look of disbelief. "It seems unlikely, since the flash would set the patient on fire."

"No, there's no flash. The camera has a special light on it."

"Well, my good vagabond, just the process of opening the patient up to place the camera would be deadly."

"No, that's the funny part. The camera is small enough to, um, insert it in the derriere to look around."

"The derriere? Have the French taken over the world in the future?"

"You know, the backside. Your bottom. Bum. Uh, fanny. Gluteus maximus. Badonkadonk."

"And this is done to cure a cold? Or baldness?"

"No, actually those are still a problem."

Look of shock. "Just a moment." Opens a door and calls to another doctor, who rushes in.

"This tramp here says in the future they put cameras in their tookus."

"He's a witch! Burn him!"

I will confess that I think the colonoscopy is miraculous, a wonderful tool to save lives. I just can't help seeing the process as comical. There is a formula in humor: tragedy plus time equals comedy. It may not apply here, but since I thought of it, I had to write it down, and I'm sure most of you have stopped reading by now. Anyway, if I teleported two hundred years into the future and explained it to a doctor then, perhaps that would make my point.

"I've traveled in time from 2021 to talk to you about colonoscopy."

"Why are you dressed like a tramp? Was there another depression I missed?"

"What is it with you doctors? This is just how I look."

"So, anyway, you guys are still sticking cameras in your tookus? Isn't that inconvenient?"

"Well, yes, but it's a necessary procedure."

"I forget, is that how you cured the cold and baldness?"

"No, those are still a problem."

Opens a door and calls to an android doctor who rushes in.

"This guy here says he's from the past, asking about colonoscopy."

"Geez, is that the thing with the leeches?"

Me: "Excuse me, I'm from 2021, not 1421."

"Is this the hilarious procedure where the doctor drives a camera around inside you and watches on a little TV? And the prep takes two days of drinking gallons of awful tasting stuff and spending hours in the bathroom?"

"Yes, that's it! I knew it would be funny. Are you still doing those?"

"Lord, no. The last doctor who did that was burned for witchcraft."

It is amazing how the medical world has progressed, and along the way introduced laughable practices like lobotomies and eating tapeworms and using heroin to treat a cough. It's easy to see them as funny now, even though they were dangerous or lethal. Well, easy for me, who somehow just dodged that lobotomy era.

Definitely take the colonoscopy seriously. And all the great diagnostics available to keep you healthy for as long as life offers you. But you have to admit the colonoscopy is funny. I'm not mocking gastroenterologists, I'm sure they are the butt of a lot of jokes. (Don't roll your eyes, you knew I was going to say it.) I am only saying that most of life is silly, even the serious parts, and all that keeps us from laughing is time or distance. Make the leap.

Hope this finds you laughing your tush off,

David

SUPER BOWL

February 2019

Greetings from the folk,

Wherein we will discuss the LIII Super Bowl, some of the strategies that led to the victory, and a breakdown of the key plays in the game. And a brief explanation of Roman numerals.

Thousands of people (literally meaning "multiple-thousands," but usually describing "more than we could count") gathered on Saturday at Gobbler's Knob, in Punxsutawney, PA to watch a critical element in the American dialogue unfold.

The town of Punxsutawney (pronounced "po-dunk") is famous for a few things, not the least of which are their incredible poor choices in naming anything, the most obvious being their own town. (See also: "Gobbler's Knob.")

The town is also famous for a cookie fundraiser at the local United Methodist church, but that hardly gets any press because of the hoopla (from the French word "Yoplait," meaning "falderal") over the previously mentioned event on Saturday.

Before we get to that, it is incumbent on us to come to an understanding about the term "folklore," or as some say, "folk lore." The word "folklore" describes how people preserve some tradition or history, usually describing an oral history; stories passed on from one generation to the next.

We still call it "folklore" because it sounds homey and friendly, like maybe we got it from the Farmer's Almanac or the Bible. Otherwise, it sounds like it's just made-up stuff, which takes all of the magic out of it, not to mention the truth.

So, the other thing that Punxsutawney, PA is famous for is Punxsutawney Phil (pronounced "fill"), who is a groundhog. Let's pause here and appreciate the fantastic coincidence that a groundhog would also have the very unusual name of "Punxsutawney" AND live in a town with the name of Punxsutawney. Let alone how weird it is that a groundhog even HAS a name.

This makes me wonder if maybe all animals have names, and all this time we have been completely ignorant of this fact. There are, seriously, at least LIII squirrels in my yard and it just boggles my mind that they may have names, aside from the generic. Not to mention the deer and the skunk, which I'm not sure why I am mentioning when I started this sentence with "not to mention."

But I digress.

On Saturday, more people than we could count showed up to see Punxsutawney Phil live out a little local folklore. Phil, as I like to call him, because I am sick to death of typing out the word Punxsutawney, as you recall, is a groundhog. At some point on February 2, Phil emerges from the ground, somehow prearranged to pop up at Gobbler's Knob. If when Phil comes up into the air he sees his shadow and retreats back into the hole, this will predict that the majority of the Oscars will be won by white men this year.

Phil has also predicted the price of gas (which goes up or down depending on if he sees his shadow or not) and also has predicted for two years in a row that the Mexican government will not pay for a border wall. If he pops out of the ground and sees his shadow, according to folklore, it means that the unemployment rate will decline. Also, that we will have several more weeks of winter.

This year, the folks in Punxsutawney were approached by the organizers of the Super Bowl to be part of their pregame programming, wherein Punxsutawney Phil would predict the winner of the professional football championship. If Phil did not see his shadow, then the Patriots would win, and if he did see it, then the Rams would take the trophy — and several more weeks of winter.

This is not to say that the game is fixed; that would be a tragedy, dissolving the thrill of the game, not to mention nullifying millions of dollars in Super Bowl Square gambling in office pools everywhere.

The purpose of having Phil make any predictions is mostly for entertainment value, not unlike a football referee trying to enforce rules about excessive violence in a particular play. Phil (which is not really his name, it's Carl, but lacks the alliteration we all wish we had), really is like the color commentators from CBS, only he makes his remarks the day before. So to speak, since he does not literally speak.

Anyway, I meant to spend more time reviewing the game but they are sounding the two-minute warning here (a football reference to endear me to the fans), and since I fell asleep at halftime owing to the fact that there were only three points on the scoreboard and Maroon 5 was singing, I will have to defer to more qualified observers of the game, which would likely include this squirrel in my backyard, whose name turns out to be Flushing Frank.

Hope this finds you folklored,

David

MAX RULES

May 2010

Greetings from the top of the food chain,

There are a few universal truths that are worth writing about. One is that every dog wants to go in the car with you so he can hang his head out the window. If there was an atmosphere on Mars, I am positive that dogs there would hang their heads out the windows of Martian cars going to the grocery store. No, NASA has not yet proven there are grocery stores on Mars.

The other truth is that every dog wants to sleep in your bed. I don't care what kind of dog you have, or what kind of training he's had, or if you have a waterbed or a Tempur-Pedic mattress. If he is not already, given the chance, he will sleep in your bed.

In the face of this universal truth, I present an unbreakable rule established in the great Dog Negotiation of 2002: Our dog Max will never sleep in my bed.

Max is deaf. He lost his hearing at a young age, so he has developed his other senses to compensate. One of those is the sense of sleep. He is the Zen Master of sleep.

Max sleeps on the couch, on the backs of chairs, in the window seat, on the floor, in the yard. He can sleep through anything now, and regularly does, falling asleep at almost any time in nearly any environment. But never, not under any circumstances, is he allowed to sleep in my bed. It's an ironclad, no exceptions, non-negotiable, deal-breaker, Cold War-caliber rule.

Max has always been an independent dog. Not exactly aloof, but not the kind of dog that really needs cuddling. Now that he is deaf, his independence borders on aristocratic superciliousness. This has worked out well for both him and me since he is on a Visitor's Visa as far as I'm concerned. His autonomous attitude has protected our tenuous relationship; I don't try to get him to chase a ball, and he doesn't try to sleep with me.

When he is not sleeping, Max is a watchdog. His main function is to sit at the window and watch, primarily for the UPS truck, which he has been bred to protect us from QVC deliveries. He also protects us if a rabbit or squirrel comes into the yard, at which time he barks at it until we go deaf. Before he lost his hearing, Max also barked at the toilet when it flushed. Go figure.

I'm of the opinion that dogs are not really capable of emotions. They are a knot of ON/OFF switches primarily flipped by two instincts: eating and sleeping. Ok, maybe four switches, but this is a family show.

I have not analyzed the progression, partly because I don't have insight into the mythical dog psychology, and mainly because I don't care, but at some point, Max's "I want to sleep in your bed" switch clicked over to ON.

Because he is small and has a gimpy leg, Max could not jump up on our bed without looking pathetic, so instead, he would ask me to help him. He does not speak English, so he uses another form of communication. Lurking.

Max would come into our room at night and sit next to my bed and stare at me. The kind of stare that can burn holes right through a goose-down pillow that one might choose to hide behind. After that, piercing into my REM sleep state was no problem. The message he was boring into my head: I want to sleep in your bed. I countered by taking Ambien.

Some nights, he would clear his throat as if to say "ahem." I responded by locking him in the laundry room. Nature then provided Max with the ability to adapt. Somehow, while I was at work each day earning enough money for thyroid medicine for our dog, he was at home practicing jumping up on my bed. I'm pretty sure the theme to *Rocky* was playing.

Max was no longer asking my permission to get on the bed. He would jump up and sleep there all day in preparation for sleeping there at night. And so, the first invasion stage was set. Max began appearing at my bedside in the night, and then leaping into bed and curling up at my feet. I would push him off, escort him out by the collar, and close the bedroom door.

Then came the pre-emptive stage. Max would beat me to bed, claiming prime real estate before I got there. I began going to bed at 7:30 just so I could have my own blanket. I could feel control slipping away.

One night I woke up and he was standing on the mattress looking down at me. If I didn't know him better, I might have assumed he had sinister canine intentions. In fact, he was waiting for me to scoot over so he could lie down with his head on the pillow.

Aside from the inconvenience of having to negotiate for space on my Serta, the worst thing about this development is that Max laughs in his sleep. It's a sort of chortle, actually. I think he is dreaming about sleeping in my bed, despite the unbreakable rule. Having the last laugh.

Dogs that sleep in your bed do not care what shape you have to take to sleep around them. And there's nothing you can do about it. The phrase "Let sleeping dogs lie" comes from the fact that their body weight increases by 1000 times when they fall asleep. Once a dog is asleep in your bed, the only way to move him is to bring in a crew of burley men with a winch. Or a bagel with peanut butter.

To add to the insult, Max does not sleep through the night. He gets up and steps on my groin area to make sure I'm awake, then jumps down, roams the house, checks all the windows for the UPS truck, and comes back to wake me again to tell me to move over.

Almost every morning when I get home from running, I come into the bedroom to find Max sleeping in my spot, head on the pillow, and, strangely, the blanket pulled around him. If he wakes up, which he rarely will, he does not even raise his head, just looks at me as if to say: "Allow me to demonstrate what I think of your unbreakable rules." Dog lips do not form into a smirk, but that would be redundant anyway.

I can feel the last semblance of control in my life slipping into the mist. The illusion that I am the alpha male, the lead dog, the big kahuna, slips a little each time I fill Max's dog dish, or pay his vet bill, or find him curled up on my freshly laundered clothes. And right now, he is stretched out between my high-count sheets, his head on my goose-down pillow, smugly snoring, dreaming about the day when he will write his own weekly column.

With this, I can see a day coming when our dogs will be driving our cars, heads out the window, and we will be left tied to the tree in the backyard, barking at UPS trucks.

Hope this finds you in your place,

David

David Scott Smith

GLOBAL WARMING MY COFFEE

August 2015

Greetings from the bean counter,

I like to think I am a well-informed adult. It's probably not true, but I like to think it. I will say that I listen to NPR because the voices sound so serious they must be saying something important.

But to be honest, I tend to zone out when it comes to Global Warming, capitalized here to emphasize the distinction from regular global warming, which no one believes in.

I have a pretty good grasp of what's going on, but for a variety of indefensible reasons, all of which fall under the short-sighted/selfish/nationalistic category, I don't think about it much. There is methane and ozone layer and something about rainforests, and for some reason it's making winters harder in Michigan, but it's still called "warming."

Sure, I can imagine how difficult it would be if the sea level rose and some faraway island country got submerged, which would be very inconvenient for a bunch of people I don't know. And then there are all of those glaciers, which are either melting or not melting. I forget what that was about. I read National Geographic, but just for the pictures.

I've taken a hands-off approach to this problem, sort of like looking at a toilet paper roll that is just about empty. Described best as, "I hope someone can fix this before it matters to me."

All of that changed with two little words. Coffee.

Before I go any further, you should know that I have very strong feelings about coffee. Coffee is very important to me; I divide my life into "Sleep" and "Coffee." If there was a Coffee Party in the U.S., I would be voting for whomever they nominated. Even Juan Valdez, who may be slightly under-documented.

I love coffee. The aroma, the feel of the cup in my hand, the steam rising from the dark liquid, the first sip: nutty, rich, life-giving. If you think this seems a little intense for a mere beverage, you are probably a tea drinker. Anyway, my passion for coffee has now driven me to pay attention to world events, so in yet another way, it has made me a better person.

I have been subtly impacted by the eco/social/political influences involved with coffee. I go along with free-range, fair-trade, shade-grown, GMO-free, handpicked, responsibly packaged coffee beans. Sure, I say, I'll have a cup of that organically grown Arabica, just as long as it's fresh and hot and in my hand before I feel the need to check my phone for email.

This week I was flipping past some complicated-looking graph in a magazine and stopped when I saw the word "Coffee," capitalized here because it could be a religion. The pictures in the graph showed that coffee is the second-largest commodity traded in the world, right behind oil. Fifty-two million pounds of coffee are consumed every day. One hundred million people are dependent on the coffee industry. All of that is just window dressing to give the story some body on which to hang the main message: Global Warming may affect the production of coffee. My coffee.

Something something . . . climate change . . . something something . . . rust on the leaves . . . something . . . Central America . . . something something . . . fifty percent reduction in the area suitable for growing coffee by 2050.

You don't have to be a genius to read between the lines and see the importance of that message. It means there could come a day when I can't have coffee. Yes, it appears it is some distant date, maybe when I am nearly 100, but trust me, if there is still coffee around, I will still be alive.

No coffee or, worse, bad coffee because of Global Warming? We have to DO something!

Humans were made to drink coffee; why else would our digestive system work the way it does, transforming this magic elixir into instant energy, creativity, productivity, and attractiveness? Whatever your beliefs, you must see that we were created to be in partnership with coffee. If Global Warming, or as it will now be known, Coffee Climate Change, is impacting the critical connection between man and bean, we must act.

We are stewards of this planet, all of us. We should all understand how important it is to preserve the beauty and richness of our environment. We must start today to change our behavior so that the future of our planet is ensured.

Ride your bike. Walk to the store and bring your own bags. Stop using air conditioning and flying in planes. Recycle. Do whatever you can to reduce your carbon footprint. We must do it for the billions of people we share this caffeinated space with. For the generations of our children who deserve a chance at a well-made cappuccino. Do it for the animals and plants that could be saved from extinction. Do it for the future of our planet and for the future of humanity.

But above all, do it for me. I need my coffee. If I can't have coffee, no one will be happy. And you want to be happy, right? So really, this is for you, too.

Hope this finds you brewing,

David

PAINTING WITH BEES

August 2018

Greetings from the meander,

Today I will share with you three things. I am mentioning this in case you want to get a piece of paper to keep track.

We are in the process of shrinking our house and then restoring it to nearly the exact dimension as previously. We are doing this by first removing a tiny fraction of an inch on the exterior, which will then be replaced by a virtually identical layer. The actual shape of our house will not change. At all. It will be just like David Copperfield was here and made the entire thing disappear, slightly, and then reappear.

It can be a challenging process. There are ladders involved, often poised in precarious positions, and here I am using the word "precarious" as a synonym for "perilous" and not to refer to the Pre-Carious era during which insects ruled the world. Which would be ridiculous for two reasons.

And so, I find myself at the top of a ladder, from which height I can vividly imagine reversing my vertical progress at an accelerated rate, ending suddenly on the ground next to the tool that I meant to take with me when I first ascended.

Therefore, there are ladders and tools and cursing, which are employed to slowly and carefully remove the epidermis of our house like peeling the shell off a hard-boiled egg. And then, in an even more elaborate process, putting the shell back on in an almost exact replica of the first shell. Maybe a slightly less reddish color, but not too yellow.

So that's one thing. Here is the second thing.

Informed citizens already know there is a bee shortage. Farmers across the country have raised the issue to a meme-worthy Facebook post, which clearly shows the crisis in a way informed citizens can comprehend. With the bee shortage, many crops are in danger of not being pollinated. There is a simple reason for this bee shortage; they are all living inside my house.

The more time I spend on ladders shrinking my house, the more places I find where bees are living. Some have formed nests, which are obvious, but many of them, and when I say "many" I mean "all of the bees in the Northern Hemisphere," have taken up residence inside.

Like most things that do not contribute to me getting coffee, I try not to think about bees. I have always assumed they have a similar attitude about me.

If I find they have built an elaborate mud fort behind a shutter I am taking off the house so that later I can put it back exactly where it was in the exact dimension it was, but in a slightly different color, I remain ambivalent. Until one of the bees stung me right in my cartilage.

It turns out bees do have an opinion about my existence, and it is not as neutral as I have often assumed. This rancor, obviously welling for some time, inspired one of their ranks to stab me in the cusp of my ear.

What I have surmised is that the bees resent having to work for farmers for free. That antipathy, buzzing slightly below the surface of their seemingly carefree existence, can lead to violence. Which, for the record, I did not reciprocate, at least not very effectively.

And so, because of this agricultural oppression, there has been a mass migration of bees to occupy the internal shape of my house, which, as previously mentioned, I am currently shrinking/growing from the exterior shape.

It is in this context I find myself at the top of a ladder, which is swaying from the pull of the moon and through which I can feel the vibration from the shifting of the tectonic plates. Defying the laws of gravity and common sense, I am attempting to slice off a thousandth of an inch of the outside of my house. And in that moment a bee drifts by, as if to say, "Are you sure you want to be up here?"

Those of you who got a piece of paper to keep track will have noted that of the three things I said I would share, only two have been noted so far. And that is the third thing.

Hope this finds you busy as a bee,

David

SPORGATORY

June 2020

Greetings from the stands,

A few months ago, when things began to shudder under the weight of Covid, one of the early casualties of normality was spectator sports. Naïvely, I believed that the juggernaut of televised sports would resist. When billions of dollars are at stake and a nation of rabid fans are waiting to be distracted, I felt certain that somehow sports would continue.

But I was wrong. Admitting I was wrong about something I don't know anything about is not an earth-shattering revelation. Here I was going to insert a sports metaphor for how little I know about sports, but you can see my conundrum. Perhaps just that last sentence says it all.

Crowds evaporated and so did the players who performed for them. There were some weak attempts at sports in empty venues, but that was just sad. And prompted the existential question: If a ball drops in a stadium and there is no one to see it, is it fair or foul?

And so, we moved into this unprecedented sports purgatory, now a trademarked era called "Sporgatory."

According to scientific research, which may be invented by me for this paragraph, the human brain has evolved from the primitive hunter/gatherer phase to the more advanced watcher/eater stage. This development aligned perfectly with the advent of spectator sports, which connects with the need to ingest hot dogs and hoagies while seeing athletes perform arcane gyrations.

Just as we as a species have reached the apex of our development, sports were removed from our world. It has created a void in the collective fan-psyche. Sports fans have done their best to fill the need, watching the talking heads review stats from the last games, now months old, and making predictions about trades between teams that are currently on hiatus. Hiatus, as you know, is an island off the coast of Florida where millionaire athletes shelter their endorsement income.

Of course, it's not just hard for the spectators; the athletes have suffered too. (Pause here to consider support groups for sad millionaires.) Some diehard fans (not fans of the Christmas movie, I mean dedicated sports nuts) have taken to wearing their logos on their Covid masks to show support. (Google: "millionaire's lives matter.")

Recently, the Chinese Professional Baseball League started its season. One team, the Rakuten Monkeys (not made up by me for humor purposes) is filling the stands with robotic mannequins so that the players don't feel silly as they perform, particularly while arguing with umpires. The robots are programmed to boo the Monkeys whenever they make a bad play. (Boo The Monkeys may be a perfect name for the next great rock band and/or software company.)

Hope This Finds You

There is no way of knowing when the pandemic will fade to the point that sports can return to filling the stands with happy fans booing their favorite teams. There has been some talk about having the teams play spectatorless. There is already some experimentation with this concept over the last decade or so, including WNBA games, cricket matches, spelling bees, whittling competitions, and curling and caber toss tournaments. (Curling and caber toss are not actually one event, but that would definitely boost viewership if they were.)

Recently we visited my mother-in-law, who introduced us to her friend Hilda, a spry 90-something who lives next door. I was told that Hilda loves sports, all kinds, watches everything. I said to her that it must be hard now, with the dearth of athletic events. She chuckled a little and said that she watches reruns of all the games. She is losing her memory, so she can't remember if she has seen them before or how it turns out. So it's all the same excitement to her.

It's possible that Hilda has achieved the apex in sports maven evolution. I will say, parenthetically (but without the use of parentheses), that Hilda has forgotten more about sports than I ever knew. At any rate, I can imagine that any real sports aficionado would envy her place in fan development. To her, every game is exciting, every play is breathtaking, and every score is the winning point.

In some ways, it may be a place to aspire to for anyone, including the sports atheists, among whom I am numbered prominently. (Numbered Prominently may also be the perfect name for the next great rock band/software company.)

Hope this finds you purgatorial,

David

Hope this finds you imagining

"Everything you can imagine is real."

Pablo Picasso

BARN

February 2021

Greetings from the sweetness,

My father would carry me across the hardpack yard toward the big red outbuilding with the gambrel roof, and I would point and call out, and he would laugh and swing me around. It felt as if I were flying.

My brother Ethan would tell people: "We call him Barn because it was the first word he said, and the only word he said until he was almost five." My parents named me Wilson; I don't remember what they called me, since both of them died of fever when I was young. After that, Ethan took care of me, and to him I was always Barn.

When I was old enough to help around the farm, I would follow Ethan into the fields and help move hay bales and dig post holes. When there wasn't enough work for me, Ethan would let the neighbors hire me for extra money. I would stand there, mute, while Ethan arranged things.

"This here's Barn, he's strong, but he's harmless. Just tell him what to do, and he'll do it." I waited, looking at my boots, wishing I had a way of saying the words in my head. I did the work and touched my cap as a thank you when I was paid and went back to our farm.

At night, when the last chores were done, Ethan would sometimes go into town and I would sit in the front room and read. I don't know if anyone ever knew I could read: Ethan didn't ask, and I didn't explain it. I read everything that our parents had on the bookshelf, and everything else I could put my hands on. When Ethan went to the next town over for seed or some other thing, I would go to the little library there and sit with the books. It was there I found a book on bees.

Ethan let me take care of the hives. We kept bees out on the other side of the garden, where the wind was held back by a row of trees and low shrub. After our other chores, I could spend whatever time I wanted there. It was a place without struggle, where my thoughts were clear.

"He is a wonder, Barn is, with those bees. He don't even wear the net anymore, or even smoke 'em to harvest the honey," Ethan would say. "They just let him be, don't ever sting him even."

I worked among the bees, cleaning, dealing with mites and mold, scraping the combs, pulling the honey. The hives were healthy, and I poured dozens of jars to sell at the fruit stand at the end of our lane. The honey was good, sweet proof of the beauty of my time with the bees. They became my friends, of sorts, and their place in the world was one of peace, of beauty. And there was one other thing; a sense of passion I didn't know before.

I sat at the kitchen table intending to say this to Ethan: "There is a magic time in the morning when the sun is not yet the sun, but only a promise of fresh light. There is mist in the low places and everything is glistening with dew. The sky is a rare shade of blue, a reflection of the cornflowers in the grass. The bees are quiet in their home, holding each other warm, surrounded by the cool morning. And then when I sit outside there, they come out, one by one, and greet me. And I know, in Her time, She will join me there in the clover."

But the words I say are: "Go to bees now."

"Go to bees, Barn," Ethan says. "But you get these dishes cleaned up first. Hear?"

For the first year, I watched Her with the others, the drones She shared the air with. They swept and darted, whirled into shapes blurred by motion, clouds of life. I noticed Her because of the grace and power She held as She flew. She was the queen; I knew Her role with the others, knew of the relationship and the duty. I also knew She was made for more than either.

In every moment there is something, a part of us waiting to be. Even as we consider it, it is becoming part of us. Wondering brings us to wonder.

The summer of the second year, She flew to me and waited for the others to fall back. She hovered around me, sometimes holding so close I could feel the wings press the air against my eyelashes. She lighted on my hand and walked among the hair on my skin. I felt Her touch the beads of sweat, felt Her exploring me. And then She lifted into the air, hovered in front of me, and looked into my eyes. I can still feel the touch of Her and sense Her making a space in me.

It was nearly another year passed before She spoke to me. She said Her name, but it was not language, it was a sensation, a whorl of experience and beauty and emotion. It was the same way I felt words in my head, but this was more visceral, something I knew in my entire being.

The wonder seeps into our language, our desire, what we dream of, hope for. It simmers in the pulse of our bodies; it whirls the feathers in our core. Each time I came to the hive and saw Her float out to meet me, I was held in awe that defied definition.

She spoke, asked gentle questions, somehow understood my answers. She told stories of the seasons, of the way life mingled with Her, of how She saw each day through a sense I hadn't known existed, an awareness that startled me. And then one day I felt Her touch lightly on the edge of my ear, felt Her wings rest, and I heard Her soft whisper. "Wilson."

Spring was long off. The almanac told me that it would be late, the days would stay cool, and I knew the bees would be fussy, trapped inside in the brisk February mornings. I sat outside the hive and busied myself with mending one of the wooden frames, and then I saw Her rise up out of Her home.

She made Her way on the air until She was near enough to speak, and we exchanged our morning pleasantries. I felt easier inside, and at the same time my heart quickened. She waited, and then said my name, and then came close enough so that I felt Her, and She kissed me.

There will never be a need for me to tell anyone what this was, and that's just as well, since there are no words that will serve. In the fraction of a second that we became one being, there was a new creation, a new future, and with it a new kind of wonder.

From somewhere else I watched Ethan find Wilson lying in the grass. His clothes were damp, his arms and legs cast open like he had no bones. His face was relaxed and there was the slightest hint of a smile, although his lip was swollen, a little distorted from the sting. I saw Ethan slump with despair, but I also sensed his relief. He placed his hand on his brother's eyes and closed them.

I floated with Her in the air above. We embraced the morning, held it in our wings, and caressed the light the sun shared. We lifted higher, danced among the tiny buds in the branches, felt the world changing. We exchanged the wonder in our souls, and we each became something new.

And now we are a Wonder. Something beautiful and unique, the Two of Us a marvel of love, a treasure among the Wonders. We flew into the limitless next moment, which is where you will find us forever, and forever, and for all of whatever comes after.

Hope this finds you flying,

David

SUPERPOWER STORE

October 2011

Greetings from my secret identity,

The sign on the door said "Open," but the building hinted otherwise. No lights shone inside, no sign of anyone around, dried leaves gathered in drifts around the door. It was a narrow storefront, three panels of glass, frosted halfway up to obscure the interior. The small wooden sign bolted to the brick below the glass had two words: Superpower Store.

I pushed the door open, heavy wooden frame, leaded glass, so heavy I only got the door partway open and had to reset my feet to push the rest of the way in.

The man behind the counter was leaning on his elbows, head down over a newspaper, idly flipping the pages. In one hand he held an unlit cigarette.

"Afternoon," I said, walking across the wooden floor, the boards creaking. "Kinda quiet here today." I ran my hands over some boxes on the counter and looked at the dust on my fingers.

The man looked up. "Yah. Usually Halloween is packed, but funny, all the kids want to be 'Angry Birds' or Sara Palin. Not much call for all this." He waved one hand vaguely at his inventory and went back to his paper.

"Yeah." I forced a little laugh, which sounded forced and little. "So, you sell . . . uh . . ."

"Superpowers. Yessss, you can say it. If you're in here, it's not a joke. Yes, I sell superpowers. What'd you have in mind?" He licked his thumb and turned a page.

I smiled a little sheepishly, watched my toes for a minute. "Well, I don't know, I just …"

"You know, don't kid me," he said, not looking up from his paper. "Look, all the good stuff is mostly taken; invisibility, elasticity, telekinesis, along with being able to leap tall buildings." He looked up suddenly. "And don't even ask me about X-ray vision."

"Ok, ok!" I said and I held my hands out in defense and looked directly at him. "That's too bad. I was kind of hoping, maybe, that I could turn into fire, or run super-fast. Maybe have incredible strength." The memory of the front door taunted me.

He leaned on his hands now, stuck his chin out a bit as he talked. "You guys all want to be heroes or something. Superpowers won't make you heroic. If you're a jerk, you just become a super jerk."

I waited for a second, pressing my lips, trying not to say the first thing on my mind. "Seems like you should know me a little better before you insult me," I said, already wishing I had a superpower of some lethal ilk. Wishing I didn't already think he was right.

"Sorry, I just get a little . . ." he was shaking his head. He waved the unlit cigarette at me as an explanation. "Well, I can show you what I've got. I might have something'll fit."

I glanced around the room, hooks holding leather helmets, wings, metal breastplates, bright uniforms on hangers, and capes everywhere. I almost pointed to a shark fin cap.

He pawed around behind the counter and then brought out a cardboard box, flipped open the flaps, and pulled out a costume with a bold "I" on the front. My heart skipped a beat.

"How about this?" he said. "Ironic Man." He looked at me and smiled. "Only problem with this superpower is you're always explaining yourself, it's kind of a pain." My shoulders drooped, hoping for invincibility.

He slid the box aside and pulled out a smaller box with bright orange gloves. "This is pretty cool; these gloves give you the power to hold really hot objects in your hands."

I pulled them on and felt no real difference in my powers. "Aren't these just potholders?" I asked. He shrugged. I was growing impatient, wishing Apple had a superpower franchise.

"What are those boxes in that big pile?" I asked. Dozens of identical boxes stood stacked nearly to the ceiling.

"Kinda forgot about those; not many people ask about those superpowers." He pulled a few boxes and held them up to the light to read the label. "This one is 'Patience.' I remember selling a lot of those, but not lately. And this one," he held up another larger box in his other hand, "this one is 'Compassion.' Not many orders for these either. Comes with an Empathy Cape." He looked at me, his eyebrows up hopefully.

I waited, still hoping for something incendiary, or involving laser vision or blades that shot from my wrists, or time travel, or anything super-duper.

"Well, now, here we go. Here's some that I think would work for you," he said. "Odd, these always get returned by little kids, never really understood why. Right about when they become teenagers and want X-ray vision." He chuckled.

He turned the small box around and showed it held a signet ring with the letter "A" on it.

"What is it?" I asked, hoping for Astral Projection or something.

"I should warn you, this is a superpower many people cannot handle right at first. It is hard, especially for guys your age. You have to take it slow, give yourself some time to adjust. I'm just letting you know; it changes things."

I felt something run up my spine and tickle the hair on the back of my neck, and my heart rate climbed. "What is it? What superpower does it have?" I almost whispered.

"Awe," he said, holding the ring out toward me.

Just holding it, I could feel my first reaction slip away, feel the cynical impulse ebb, the sarcastic thought disappear. I slipped the ring on my finger and something tipped over in my head, and my vision blurred, and then became clear, almost painfully clear.

The room suddenly was brighter, the sound of the ceiling fan louder, the warmth more intense. The man behind the counter seemed taller; I noticed him. There was a look on his face that was not there before, a subtle look of wisdom.

I looked at my hands with wonder, the intricate lines, the incredible coordination of sinew, muscle, and bone as they worked together, flexing, the ring glinting in the light, a perfect fit on my finger.

Shadow and light stood out to astonish me, every texture, every mote of dust in the air, every cobweb was miraculous. I stood in the middle of the shop looking around me in wonder, and I found I was holding my breath.

I moved toward the door and could not wait to see how it opened, and then felt the fresh crisp air rush in around me, the smell of the season, the feel of change in nature. Sounds came pouring into me, astonishing. I could almost see the waves in the air from a car honking its horn.

"Wow," I said, my voice with a new timbre I had never felt.

The man from the store was next to me, his hand on my shoulder, his other hand holding out a pair of chrome-plated goggles, a tiny "A" embossed on them. "You may want these at first," he said. "Blocks out a little of what you see. It's too amazing out there to take it all in at once." I took the goggles and let them dangle from my fingers.

I stepped out into the street and watched the world unfold in front of me, the incredible colors in the trees, the cotton sky, the complexity of the plants, the richness of the brick, the grain in every piece of wood. Architecture stood out, the plan and order and creativity of someone expressed in the buildings around me.

I walked for miles, astonished, my mouth open, unable to express myself at the wonder around me, nature, things growing, evolving, passing on, and becoming part of the next things. People moving, interacting, expressing, each of them miraculous, almost impossible to believe. I felt the gentle rush of the earth spinning beneath me, gravity holding me in perfect balance.

"Wow," I whispered. I blinked and the world rushed back at me, and I knew I would never want to go to sleep, never go inside, never leave this moment.

I felt the connection between things, the sense of it, the beauty in flaws, understood that I did not need to understand what laughter meant, the purpose of black holes, and the origin of anything; only that it existed, and it poured into me and around me and I could feel it lifting me.

I opened my arms wide, felt the air course by me, and I flew into creation.

Hope this finds you powerful,

David

CUPID

February 2012

Greetings from the quiver,

"You can't bring weapons on board."

"It ain't actually a weapon . . ."

Sara could not hear what was said after that, because the bus driver had stepped down out of the doorway, blocking the sound for a moment, and their voices were muffled. She could make out their shapes at the side of the bus, the driver putting something in the luggage bay underneath.

She watched him come down the aisle and felt something changing, and she was afraid and not afraid at the same time.

He braced himself on the seats as he came through the bus; she could see he was lean, moved with a powerful grace. He had long hair, pulled back and tied but falling loose over his face now, streaked with gray, greasy and coarse. He wore blue jeans, cuffed over cowboy boots, torn and dirty, and a mechanic's shirt with the sleeves cut off. There was a name embroidered above the pocket; "Chet."

"Please don't sit here, please don't sit here, please, please . . ." Sara didn't realize her lips were moving as she said it under her breath, but then caught him looking at her mouth, and she stopped whispering. She put her magazine on the seat next to her and looked out the window.

His voice was like hearing rusty metal grating on the air as he spoke, low and harsh. "This seat taken?"

She looked at him and looked down quickly, shaking her head and picking up her magazine to make room. He sat down and she breathed in the smell of cigarettes and sweat.

She pulled her coat a little closer and glanced at his arm, saw the tattoo on his shoulder, a heart with an arrow piercing it. No name, no words.

They lurched forward away from the curb, and she tried to settle back without touching him, watching him out of the corner of her eye, taking in the weathered skin, the creased, unshaven face.

The bus maneuvered through the city, shuddering in third gear each time it slowed for traffic, and soon the passengers fell into the rhythm of travel. Sara tried to keep to her side of the bench seat, not making contact with the man. Another hour crept by, and she felt both of them relax, her own shoulders lowering, her hands unclenching. She glanced at him and saw he was looking past her out the window.

"So, are you traveling for business?" she asked.

"I'm retired," he said simply, his face not moving in the dim light.

She said without looking at him, "You are awfully young for retirement."

"I'm a lot older than I look," he said with a short laugh, and picked a flake of tobacco from his tongue.

She looked out the window as the bus prowled through the darkness, the window opaque from the humidity on the inside. She absently touched the glass and traced her finger in the moisture, realized she had drawn a heart. She stared at it for a moment.

"What's his name?" came the rasping voice next to her, startling her to look at him.

"What?" She realized she had been holding her breath. "Whose name?"

"Him. The guy you're not with," said the man. He motioned with his chin at the glass.

Sara did not answer. She was not going to talk to this man, this ragged retired bus vagabond. She was not going to open up and talk about this now with a Trailways stranger.

"His name is Zane," she said. Anyway.

The man waited for a moment, his hands at rest on his knees. "What's he do, this Zane guy?"

She looked at the man again, wanting to tell him it was none of his business, and could not. "He owns a used record store. Just sells old LPs and 45's, just vinyl."

"There money in that?" the man asked.

Sara looked away. "I don't know. He just likes music, likes the feel of the LPs. It's kind of his passion." Her laugh trailed off into a sigh. "He's hoping it takes off; he's in this little hole in the wall on Lafayette, downtown by the convention center."

"'Grooves,'" he said.

She turned in her seat to face him. "You know him? You know Zane?"

"Nah, but I know where he's at."

The man stretched his arms out in front of him, ropes of muscle and sinew shaping his skin and she saw the scars on him, long jagged tears, as if some animal had gotten hold of him. Sara felt a shiver in her.

"So, you don't have to say, but why ain't you with Zane?"

She bit the inside of her cheek, to keep from crying. Twisting her fingers together in her lap, she looked back out the window through the shape she had drawn, the condensation running in drips over her artwork, like tears through her own heart.

"I don't know," she said, wishing she would stop talking now, but wanting to tell someone, wanting it not to be just her that wondered. She turned her head to him. "I wanted to be with him, but it's all mixed up, he doesn't seem to get it."

"You love him," the man was not asking.

Sara looked at him. "I feel it, it's pretty strong in me, but it isn't that clear for him."

"Some people know it, some don't, some don't want to know it," the man said. "Some got to be shown."

She told him things then, all of them. It poured out of her, how she met Zane, how they went on for weeks, "running into each other" at the coffee shop, until she practically forced him to ask her out. She told him how she fell for him, from the first time he played his favorite record, told him about their first kiss when the entire world disappeared.

The man said nothing, just looked at her, and she felt like something had just opened up, like a black hole, with a pull so powerful that it was beyond nature to resist. And she told him how they tried living together, and she felt like she was putting it all on the line, and he seemed like he was hedging. And how yesterday it was too much.

"I don't know how we can get by, living over the shop, and eating ramen noodles, and . . . and I said maybe I should go back home." She looked down at her magazine, the cover turning to a mosaic now. "I could feel him wanting to tell me to stay, and . . . he just never did." She snorted a little, the cry starting in earnest now, and the first tear broke free and landed on the magazine.

The man put his hand on hers, and she was not startled. His hand was coarse, but he cupped her hand gently, and she could feel his strength. It was neither warm nor cold. It was exactly the temperature of her own skin. Just above his wrist there were two wings tattooed on his scarred forearm.

She pointed at the wings. "Were you, like, in the army, or . . ."

The man smiled, showing a chipped front tooth, and cracked lips.

"Naw, darlin', I ain't dangerous enough for that. I'm a lover, not a fighter." He laughed quietly, but from deep in his chest, and it sounded like some primal growling. "But you know what Pat Benatar said … " He chuffed a short laugh, "'Love is a battlefield.'"

Sara felt her heart slow again. The tears stopped and she wiped the last sniffle with her sleeve. She rested her head back against the seat and waited for a moment. She smiled at him, looking at him now, seeing the blue eyes, the baby's face under the creased, scarred skin. "I'm Sara," she said, "And you must be Chet."

He laughed again, "Well honey, I ain't Chet, but that'll do." He reached up over her head and pulled the Emergency Stop button. "And . . . right here is where we say goodbye."

The light and buzzer went off and the bus braked, people in the seats around them muttering questions to each other as the driver made his way into the shoulder. The man stood up in the aisle and gathered his hair behind his head, twisting the coarse mess behind his head and tying it off.

"You got a cell phone?" he asked her.

She cringed, wondering if he was going to ask for her number. She nodded her head imperceptibly, her eyes now locked on his.

"Is it on?" he asked.

She nodded again.

"Awright," he said to her, lowering his head down beneath the overhead bin. His voice thrummed at her, so deep she could feel it in her chest. "I'm stepping out of retirement for one last time. When I do, it's going to unleash something, and you better brace yourself."

He smiled and reached down and touched her cheek. "Some got to be shown, but once they see it, there's no turning back."

Sara felt the shiver again and saw the spark flash in his blue eyes. "Sara. I ain't doin' this twice. So don't miss it."

The driver stood in the aisle behind the man. "What the heck, man, this is the middle of nowhere." The man turned in the aisle and Sara could see the muscles ripple through his shirt, and watched him fill up the space between the seats, taller now. The driver backed up a step.

She watched him swing off the bus, the driver following him down, and felt the vibration of the luggage bay being swung open. She watched the pantomime of the two of them on the dirt shoulder, the bus driver raising his hands in question, the man waving him away.

She looked out the window as the bus pulled back onto the pavement, watched him bend over his case and open it and take something out. Watched him raise it up in his hands . . . and fade from sight in the glow of the taillights.

She turned in her seat and looked out the back window and saw a flash, something arcing into the sky above the road, back toward the city. It looked like a shooting star, but . . .

She sat back in her seat, feeling lightheaded, forgetting for a moment where she was, only sensing the strength of the emotion in her. Suddenly her heart was racing again, her imagination racing with it.

And then her phone rang.

Hope this finds you answering,

David

ELEVEN MINUTES LATE

February 2004

Greetings from the last minute,

Ben was 11 minutes late for everything his entire life.

He was the last one out of bed in the morning and the last one to bed at night. His family waited for him in the car, at the amusement park, at football games and birthday parties. He was late for church, late for Cub Scouts, late for dentist appointments, late for breakfast, lunch, and dinner.

No amount of preparation would help. Shoes mysteriously disappeared, backpacks wandered off, homework reappeared at the last moment. Alarm clock tricks never worked; his inner clock would not be fooled. And regardless of when he awoke, his world would not adjust to the world waiting for him. It would have to wait.

"Hurry up Ben! For crying out loud, what are you doing?" his mother shouted from the bottom of the steps.

"I'm changing my shirt, the other one had toothpaste on it," said Ben, his arms half in the sleeves of the clean shirt. "And I can't find my viola music."

Before his mother could speak, they heard the sound of the school bus honking as it went by. They both knew that if he left now, and ran as fast as he could, he would be 11 minutes late for homeroom. His mother threw up her hands and went muttering back to the kitchen to feed his little brother.

He was late for school, late for lunch, late coming back from the library. He was late coming home and late for his viola lesson. He wasn't picked for soccer because he was late for tryouts.

As the years went by, Ben became accustomed to being late, and it rarely bothered him. He was a patient, confident, intelligent boy, and was only slightly affected by the exasperated looks of those around him. He felt bad for his parents, who seemed always in a panic about him being late. As much as he wanted to please them, there was always some other voice that distracted him, and no deadline could tempt him back.

Through high school he wandered the empty halls, his fellow students already 11 minutes into their studies. He met the janitors, the security people, the delivery men, and the cafeteria employees as they arrived. He waved goodbye to them each afternoon as he left, tromping through the flotsam of his fellow students who had already made their exit. He was a regular boy in every other way, but he was still an echo of his peers, sounding 11 minutes after they had gone on.

Ben had friends; he was a very likable kid. He was open and easy to talk to, mature beyond his years. He was philosophical about the challenges of being a teenager, optimistic about the future. Girls orbited around him, drawn to his easy manner and good looks. They found him enigmatic, unaffected by the usual pressures that weighed on young men. Unfortunately, Ben's attempts at dating were doused with the same tardiness in every other part of his life, and romance will rarely tolerate a late suitor.

The day he left for college, a neighbor had to drive him because he missed his ride when he went back to the house for a book he wanted. He arrived at his dorm 11 minutes after they gave his room to an exchange student from Paraguay. Four years later, in a strange confluence of events that included a toaster fire, a stranded elevator and a runaway pony, he missed his commencement by 11 minutes.

His counselor saw Ben's potential and arranged for a wonderful job opportunity in the city. Ben was grateful and excited at the chance to live in the city. The night before his interview, he laid out his clothes, set his alarm for an hour earlier than needed, and double-checked the times for the train the next morning.

He ran to catch his train, briefcase in hand, one blue sock, one brown sock, his coat only half on, hanging from one arm. Even before he made it to the platform, he knew the train was gone, rolled out at 8:00 a.m. sharp, just about 11 minutes ago.

He stood at the tracks, puffing a little from his run. His forehead was not creased; no sign of tension was on his face. His blue eyes scanned the train schedule on the wall and saw that he would not make it to the city in time for his interview. His job would go to some more punctual prospect.

Sixty seconds ticked by. Ben heard a noise off toward the steps and turned to see a young woman running across the platform toward the tracks. Her suitcases banged against her legs as she ran, making for a comical gait. She skidded to a stop at the apron and looked up and down the tracks, as if expecting the train to appear from either direction at that moment. Ben watched her drop the bags she was carrying and then sit down dejectedly on the concrete next to them.

To Ben, she was beautiful. The way she held herself, the long, graceful hands, her pale skin. From where he stood, he could see her eyes; even looking down, they were lively and bright. Her auburn hair framed her face, a long intelligent-looking face, right now a little creased as she rested it in her hands.

Ben walked to where the girl's bags were and waited until she noticed him. She stood up, startled and self-conscious. As soon as she looked at him, Ben smiled. She smiled back, but the smile faded.

"I was going to the city," she said gesturing at the bags around her, "I had an audition this afternoon." She shrugged; tears were welling in her eyes. Ben's heart melted.

"I missed the train," she said, "I'm guessing by about 12 minutes." She looked down at her hands and said, almost to herself, "Of course it would be 12 minutes. It always is." She wiped her eyes with the back of her hand.

Ben leaned down and set his briefcase on the concrete. As he stood up, he extended his hand, intending to introduce himself. At that moment, the girl's hand came out and, without looking, their hands met.

Ben felt as though he had been connected to some incredible force. It felt familiar and right, as though he had been waiting his whole life to touch her. He held her hand lightly, not really shaking it, but holding it. He could feel the tears on the back of her hand.

"I'm Ben." And she said, "I'm Zoe."

Ben could not think of what else to say. They stood there looking at each other, joined at the hands. Time spun on without them; minutes and hours and days and years and all of it at someone else's pace. Neither felt even a moment pass.

"Happy Valentine's Day, Zoe," Ben finally said.

Her smile grew wider, and she laughed.

"That was yesterday," she said.

Hope this finds you in time for love,

David

RED MITTENS

February 2014

Greetings from where the colors mix together,

His slippers made a raspy noise against the linoleum as he moved to the sink. Placing one cup, one bowl in the stainless-steel square, rinsing the last bits of food down the drain, he leaned on the counter for a moment and let his focus slip outside the small window over the sink.

Outside, the world had been reduced to simple contrasts. The snow blanketed everything, the sky floated gray above the dull white terrain. Trees stood in dark relief, like charcoal drawings against the ashen canvas.

It didn't matter to him; he couldn't see color now, another rite of passage into his advanced years. It snuck up on him: macular degeneration, slowly wearing away the colors in his world until all that was left was what looked like an old movie playing through his glasses.

The doctor had given him a booklet to read about it but

somehow it had gotten in the mess on the kitchen table, and he thought that maybe he had accidentally mailed it with his utility bill. He stopped worrying about it, stopped trying to name the shades he had lost.

In truth, he could still see one color.

He had to think about what day it was, couldn't be sure, and walked to the wall next to the back door where the calendar was. His insurance agent had sent it; pictures of scenery from around the state, places that tourists might go that he had never seen. He pushed his glasses further on his nose and peered at the dates; they were no help. He had started to put x's in the boxes so he would know what days had passed, but he could never recall if he remembered to do it or not.

He scratched at the gray stubble on his face, scowled at the calendar as if it were bad news sent from a stranger. It didn't really matter much what day it was, except he was going to walk to the market. If today was Sunday, the store would be closed until noon.

"It's Friday. We'll go with that," he said out loud. The kitchen responded with silence.

He sat on one of the wooden kitchen chairs and pulled on his boots; big, insulated things designed by Arctic explorers. The laces were long, meant to thread through complex loops and hooks, and then there were Velcro straps to contend with. He ignored convention and knotted the cords in a big bow and stood up.

He pulled on his winter jacket and took a hat off the little coat rack hanging on the wall. It was his favorite; a plaid cap with a fleece lining, fleece flaps that folded down over his ears when he needed. He stomped across the kitchen floor and pulled open the back door and pushed out into the bright gray.

The snow had drifted a bit over his driveway and front walk. He shoveled the walk out of habit, not that anyone used it. Not even the mailman came up to his house anymore.

He walked up the drive and opened the small door leading into the garage. Inside was his Buick, clean and dry, unused since they stopped renewing his license. He opened a small bin and pulled out a scoop, ladled up a mound of birdseed and dropped the lid again. He walked across the few yards to the edge of the house where the bird feeder was.

"Bird feeder," he snorted to himself. "Squirrel feeder is what it is." He filled the tray every day, out of habit, having long since forgotten what birds he was supposedly attracting.

He closed the garage door again and walked to the sidewalk and began his hike to the market. The snow was still drifting down, turning his glasses into blurred panes. He tucked them into his coat pocket and trudged on.

The street was quiet, any sounds dimmed by the coating of white. No one else was moving around this morning, and his were the first steps in the powder. His boots squeaked on the snow as he walked, marking his rhythm. He looked up at the stop sign, smirked, and walked on.

He was not sure how long he had been walking when he realized he had missed his turn. He had not been paying attention, his head down against the wind, eyes squinting down, his glasses tucked in useless safety. And now he looked around and didn't recognize anything in the white landscape. At that moment he realized how cold he was.

He turned in place, scanning the street for something familiar. A small twinge of fear tweaked in his chest. There was a park; he assumed that from the monkey-bars and the teeter-totter, both layered with several inches of snow like some demented pastry chef had just finished. He looked across to where a car was parked and walked that way.

It was an ice rink. He might not have noticed it or bothered to guess its purpose, except there was a woman there, gliding across the surface as if she were flying over the whiteness, her arms slightly raised as she went. She was graceful and elegant, even bundled in winter layers.

He walked to a small half wall at the edge of the rink and leaned on it. He watched her skate across the outer curve of the rink and noticed something; she wore large, red mittens. Big as oven mitts.

She skated along the oval and seemed to see him and changed direction, slowing and pointing her skates toward him. She coasted to a stop about ten feet away and stood there, balanced on steel blades, and smiled at him.

Her cheeks were tinged with red from the cold, and from the exertion, he imagined. Her lips were shaped in a ruby bow beneath a petite nose. He tried to form a sentence, but she started first.

"Good morning," she said.

"Hello," he said. Suddenly he felt awkward, as if he could not fathom what should come next.

"Some day, huh?" she said, as if winter had just been invented.

"Yeah, I guess." He looked up, glanced around like he might have missed something. He looked back at her. "It's gray," he said, shrugging.

She was watching him closely, waiting for something. She skated closer toward the wall. He could not place her age. He sensed something from her, a vibration. She seemed to be filled with life, brimming with it, a vivaciousness and energy that flowed from her.

"Well, there's more to it than gray, but you have to look for it." Laughing a little.

He was not prepared for conversation; he forgot he had stopped to ask for directions. He took out his glasses and wiped them on his coat, stalling for time. She waited. Finally, he said, "My name is

Stanley."

She paused for a moment. "Nice to meet you," she said, pulling off a mitten and extending her hand. He took it without thinking and she squeezed his hand, and the warmth flowed from her. He felt it rush up his arm and fill his chest. He looked into her eyes and felt it again.

A moment passed. And the sensation, the warmth, spread over him. He kept thinking that he should be letting go of her hand. And he could not. He forgot about being cold, about being lost. He forgot about what he forgot.

"I'm Hope," she said it like he would recognize it, as if to say, "But you knew that."

"Nice to meet you," he said, not even knowing he was going to say it.

"Stanley, your hand is frozen. You should be wearing gloves."

He frowned, remembering now he had walked out without them. He could see them, traitors, sitting on the kitchen table, warm and safe at home.

She let go of him at last and pulled off the other mitten and set them both on top of the wall next to his hands.

"Take these. I have gloves too," she said.

"No, really I couldn't take…"

"Please. Today is a day we give people gifts."

His mind fluttered; he was sure it was not Christmas. He was positive the calendar said February. He looked at her, helplessly.

"Come on Stanley. Your hands are freezing."

He reached over and picked up the mittens, fumbled them on. He had trouble finding where his thumb went. He struggled for a moment longer, self-conscious, silly that such a simple thing would be so hard. And then they were on. A perfect fit.

When he looked up, she was still smiling. He had not noticed before, but he saw the tiny lines at the corners of her eyes when she smiled. Her face told him: she had known worry, but it did not overwhelm the smile.

"Thank you for the . . . the mittens." He held them up to prove he got it right.

"You're welcome. Looks like that's your color."

He chuckled. "Yes, as a matter of fact, it is."

"So . . . do you skate?" she asked, still looking into his eyes as if she wanted to see the answer there.

He shook his head. "Not a great idea at my age," he said, wagging his head and shoulders, miming as if he were losing his balance.

She laughed. "You're funny. You just need someone to lean on while you get started."

He shrugged, not sure how to disagree.

They stood at the little wall, the winter air tugging little clouds from their lips as they talked, and then the quiet swallowing them up again. She reached to the little wall and patted his hand.

"Ok, Stanley, I'll see you tomorrow," she said, gliding backward impossibly, it seemed.

Stanley paused. "What, why . . . am I going to see you tomorrow?"

She slowed and pointed one skate point down, stopping her glide. "Because you are going to bring me hot chocolate," she said with a smile that lit her entire face. She pushed one blade into the ice and skated off.

He watched her for a moment longer, saw her wave, and then he turned to go. He looked at his footprints in the snow and decided he was bright enough to follow his own trail back home.

In his kitchen, he stood leaning against the kitchen counter, his hands cradling a cup of coffee. The mittens lay on the kitchen table, formed a perfect V, joined at the cuffs, the two oversized ovals creating a heart shape on the oak. The shape reminded him of something. He went back to the calendar hanging on the wall. The twenty-eight boxes, each with their own number.

Halfway through the month, one of the boxes held a tiny heart. Today's box. A red heart. He smiled, his face a roadmap of creases and lines. Somewhere in his chest, the warmth spread again.

He searched in the cupboard until he found the old thermos. He twisted off the top and rinsed it out and set it to dry. He needed the little cup that used to screw on the top. He pawed through the big drawer next to the Kelvinator. Spatulas, corn cob holders, a whisk, can openers. Here it is. A red cup. He set it near the thermos and thought about how to make hot chocolate.

Out of the corner of his eye, he saw movement at the window, something at the bird feeder. When he looked, it was gone. And then it was back. A yellow finch. Incredibly bright in the snowy white setting. He closed his eyes and shook his head and adjusted his glasses on his nose, then looked again. Yellow with bits of green tinged in black, the finch flitted for a moment, pecking at the feed, and then hopped to a pine branch, the deep emerald needles showing off its colors.

He watched the bird feeder a while longer. Blue jays, a cardinal, another finch, a sparrow. Little flurries of color appearing and vanishing at the window.

He sighed and let the smile come again. He picked up his coffee, watched the world fill with color, and thought about where he had put his old hockey skates.

Hope this finds you with your heart full,

David

David Scott Smith

ROOTS

February 2020

Greetings from a Maple Valentine,

They grew up together. Neither knew the day they met; they just always were there. They lived at the edge of a thick forest, close to where the river bent to explore a different way.

He noticed her first, or it seemed that way. It was autumn, and she wore colors he had never seen together, and it made something in him shiver. He willed her to notice him, but it was impossible to know what impression he made. He waited and as seasons passed, his patience grew deeper, along with his feelings for her.

The grass grew around them, small shrubs appeared, wildflowers sprouted in small places out of the wind. He watched her grow stronger, her limbs sinuous and supple, reaching out from her, caressing the air around her, reaching into the sky, holding it in place above them.

He sent her small gifts with the squirrels, who, while not known for their romantic side, were willing messengers, scurrying across the open space between them, bringing nuts, small branches, and little purple ditch flowers. She seemed unmoved.

Behind him, the pine trees chuffed coniferously and the ducks on the river laughed at his foolishness. He shook off their teasing and settled deeper into the soil to wait and wonder.

In the spring, he stretched his limbs and held out a robin's nest. A tiny construction of twigs and leaves and bits of string. In the heart of it, three brilliant ovals, the color the sky would aspire to. They were jewels, he knew, beautiful and fragile and perfect. If she noticed them, he could not tell; there was not so much as a flutter of a leaf. He settled back to wait, and the seasons whirled.

Children came down the path near the river on their way to school, crossing an arched wooden bridge a few hundred yards from the bend. They climbed the trees, shuffled through the leaves, marched on to wherever children go. In the winter, he saw a couple snowshoeing through the woods, laughing and calling to each other, their faces flush with the cold and something magic between them. He was inspired by them and looked at her to see if she felt this and saw the same thing he always saw. She was beautiful, elegant, and strong. And silent.

The two of them grew, slowly, naturally, filling up the space in the woods. Each year he felt his limbs growing toward hers, and for one season they nearly touched. But late every fall the men would come with ladders and bow saws and pruning tools and gently, kindly, trim the air between them wider.

One winter evening, two people lifted a small birdhouse and hung it from his low branch. He didn't think anything of it in the moment. But as years passed, as sparrows came and went and wrens made a home and left for other places, he felt it as an extension of him. And one day, on the edge of summer, he held it a little higher, so she would see it. For the first time in their lives, she spoke to him.

"it's beautiful," she said.

He told her the first words he thought: "you are beautiful."

The wind riffled her leaves and she swayed slightly, green glinting in the sunlight. She leaned toward him, and he felt the earth change.

He watched her on an August morning, dew on her leaves, the sky behind her pale blue, chalk dust clouds drifting over them. He ached to tell her something more, to say whatever had first resonated in him. He waited another year, and another, and one day he started to say and couldn't. She sensed him there and said, "i know."

On a late summer afternoon, he saw the sky transform, and it brought rain, which wet her leaves in a soft staccato. He watched the water sluice off her, each leaf shaking with the rain's travel. Her texture darkened as the water ran down her trunk and soaked the ground around her. He felt the rain on him too, felt it join them, held them together in the downpour, connected by tiny droplets.

They lived together at the edge of the river, together and always apart. They talked quietly of animals and insects, of the children who ran along the river. They both wondered where the river was off to, always so intent on being elsewhere, while they were content to be only there.

She would twist her twigs into small works of art, and he would draw his limbs against each other to create soft, moaning songs. She would applaud in the wind until he blushed deep green. Once in a while, a leaf of his would drift into her and she would capture it and hold it as if it were her own.

Winter came and they pulled a white blanket over them and waited, watching the river, the sun arcing over them relentlessly, knowing spring would be with them soon. The children came one morning, all of them carrying red paper hearts, laughing like the water splashing on rocks, calling to each other as they ran across the frosted bridge. They knew it was a special day.

The day brightened and he gathered a gift in his empty branches, filled every place until the boughs bent with the weight of each tiny bird. Slowly he was transformed as each one landed, filled him. He held the starlings as if his own breath, and then exhaled and they lifted from his limbs into the air around him, a living cloud. They whirled and danced and dove, and then as one living thing, descended into her, still chattering with the joy they were part of. She laughed with them, and he felt her delight hum in him.

That night when they were alone, she put the full moon in her branches, a brilliant broach that bathed them in the same light, held them together in that ivory essence. He was in awe of her.

"i love you," she said, giving him the words he had waited to know

Beneath the moon-painted snow, beneath the layer of leaves they had undressed, beneath the soil that held them, their roots wound through the earth, sought open places, and finally found one another. He felt her, felt the life in her, and she wound each tiny tendril she had around him, and felt him become part of her.

The seasons danced and decorated and left and returned, and the two of them grew taller and stronger. New children ran between them, new birds lighted in them, new leaves budded from their love and whirled into the world, and all the while their roots embraced each to the other. And each time he thought of it, no matter the season, he would lean toward her and say:

"i love you." And she knew.

"i love you," she would say. And he knew.

Hope this finds you growing together,

David

SOUL'S MATE

February 2017

Greetings from the smitten,

Julius had stopped pretending he was an out-of-work actor. Now he was an out-of-work busboy. The only redeeming part of his unemployment was his side gig, busking in the park as a living statue.

Each afternoon he would go to the park and drop his box as close as he could to the fountains, where all of the tourists eventually passed. By the time the sun set, he would clear fifty bucks.

Julius would pull out a costume from his trunk, then paint his face and hands, and for most of the afternoon he would stand perfectly still on a plywood box and resist the urge to spit on the tourists who taunted him. They would stand there and mock him, and when he wouldn't break, they put a dollar in the bucket in front of him. Sometimes loose change: it all added up.

It was not acting. But it was better than clearing dirty dishes in "Kaos" or whatever they were calling that hole in the wall they told him not to come back to. On this day, Julius was dressed as Cupid. It was not a great idea, took so long to do the body paint and he had to borrow a bow and a quiver and paint it white. He felt a little self-conscious in a toga. But he knew the tourists would love it. Especially today. There would be a lot of pictures, a lot of dollars.

No one came close for three hours. For the first time in what seemed like forever, he was going to lose money standing still. Then, out of the corner of his eye, he saw a woman walking toward him.

She was petite, moved gracefully, like a dancer, as if her life was being choreographed one step at a time. He couldn't turn his head to watch her, so he was forced to let her reveal herself. She was barefoot. Her dress was some filmy, silken fabric; the word "diaphanous" came to mind, a word he had never used in conversation. Her hair was auburn, braided close to her neck. He felt his heart begin to pick up. She was incredible.

She stood close enough for him to see the texture of her skin, the almond shape of her eyes. He waited, trying not to stare at her, keeping his focus soft so he stayed inanimate, in character. He was not the god of desire; he was a statue of the god of desire. Suddenly his mouth was dry.

He watched her looking at him. He could see a thin necklace around her neck, a small heart dangling just below the tiny hollow of her throat. Where his lips belonged. He waited, willing himself to be still, while everything else in him told him to move.

She stretched up and brought her face within inches of his. He could feel her breath on his skin when she spoke: "It's painful, isn't it? To be right there, so close to life, and unable to do what your soul screams for." She spoke softly, only he would hear. In the timbre of her voice was something primal that plucked at him in a place he hadn't known about.

Julius felt himself trembling. He could feel her eyes exploring his.

He realized he was holding his breath. And then it was too much; he blinked. And then looked into her eyes. She smiled. "There you are," she whispered.

Julius could not move. He was not pretending to be a statue; he was frozen by her, not wanting to do something that would distract her, or cause her to leave. He was not thinking about any of this, just mesmerized by the life in her eyes, a vibrancy that pulled him out of the world and into just this moment, which became his future.

Time stopped mattering. They stood in place in the middle of the plaza and the world swirled around them, and it was just a reflection of the life they created in each other's eyes. He felt something welling between them, a mixture of pain and joy, something he could only equate to music, for some reason. It was being created right in that moment. He knew she was smiling, could see the lines forming around her eyes. She took a deep breath and breathed him in.

And then she was gone. Slipped from him like water.

It took a moment for him to recover, and he looked across the plaza she was already beyond the fountains, heading toward the alley. Julius straightened, realizing where he was, and dropped his bow and leaped off the box to go after her.

He ran, stiff-legged from standing for hours, into the alley. He could see her moving through the crowd, thought he saw her look over her shoulder at him. How could she be so far away? She was not running, just moving effortlessly through the throngs of tourists coming the other way.

His heart was hammering. He saw her once more and then lost her. Now he was frantic, pushing people aside, breathless as he fought after a glimpse of her. He searched the street for an hour, finally realizing why people were staring at him, remembered he was wearing only a toga. He walked back to the plaza and saw someone had stolen his tip bucket.

The next day he walked the alley again, dressed like an out-of-work busboy. He hadn't slept, couldn't stop thinking of her, hating himself for not saying something or asking her name . . . anything but just standing there like a statue.

He circled the block, thinking that maybe she worked near there. The second time around, he found himself in front of the art museum. Without pausing, he turned in and pushed through the large glass doors. He strolled through the front lobby and into the halls, looking from side to side, not at the art but the other people there, searching for her among the docents, the gift shop clerks, the art-lovers. There was no reason to expect her there, but there was no reason not to.

He moved into the next gallery and stopped, all of him stopped. He tried to swallow and could not. She was there, in a pool of sun from the skylight above, luminescent, filled with the same energy he felt when he first saw her. Julius felt his knees weaken and he lowered himself onto a bench.

"Dancing Maiden," the small sign said. "Alberto Cambi. Italian. 19th Century."

She stood there, draped in light, her dress, the thinnest possible shape that marble could take, flowing over her like a second skin. Her hair, now Carrara white, like the rest of her, twisted into a braid against her neck. She was smiling. Barefoot, in mid-step, he could sense the movement, he could see her dancing, see her gliding as she had first moved into his sight.

It took incredible effort to stand again, as if the earth conspired to keep him in place in front of her. He moved closer, unaware of the people who stepped back to make room. He stood inches from her, saw the tiny heart around her neck, saw the shape of her eyes. Longed for the color that had been there, where now was just the carved white, the fine lines that sprung from her smile etched more than a hundred years without changing.

But even in the cold marble he could sense her. He felt the same vibration, the same warmth he knew from the day before. He could feel her breath, he could hear the sensual cello stroke in her words. And he said, "It's painful, isn't it? To be right there, so close to life, and unable to do what your soul screams for."

He leaned a little closer. Looked into her carved eyes, felt the synchronicity again, saw them look back at him.

"There you are," they said as one.

Hope this finds you waiting for love,

David

DAY AFTER OZ

February 2011

Greetings from where they really do come true,

The door had a knot of tin bells tied to the frame so as he pushed through into the diner they clattered loudly. He reached up to touch them, to quiet them.

He stepped into the diner, giving a quick glance around to see if she had arrived before him somehow. Midmorning, too early for the lunch crowd, there were only a couple of people eating. He clumped onto the tile floor wishing he were quieter, not wanting people to stare. He chose a booth where he could see the front door and slid into the vinyl bench, his joints rasping as he crouched, folding his long legs under the table.

The waitress brought coffee, a spoon balanced on the rim, a tiny metal cream pitcher. His fingers absently traced its shape as he stirred his coffee.

He watched the door. He waited, knowing that he might be waiting forever. He would wait forever. He glossed over for a moment, went in his mind to the somewhere from which he had just returned, watching the moments reel by behind his eyes. He wasn't sure how much time had passed when he heard the doorbells jangle again.

And his eyes focused on her. He felt things go crazy inside him.

She swept into the diner, all colors and textures and warmth and light and sounds, and he realized why everything he saw reminded him of her. He watched her move, already knowing exactly how every part of her would behave, having held her in his mind since the first day. And then she was at the table and settled perfectly on the seat across from him.

"You gonna want a menu, Hon?" asked the waitress

"Just coffee," she said, peeling off her coat, unspooling her scarf, and he could not imagine it being done more beautifully.

They stirred their coffee and fussed with napkins. He arranged and rearranged the ketchup bottle and the salt and pepper shakers, helpless to prevent his hands from performing.

"I heard you were back from your little adventure. Wasn't sure you'd call me," she said, a little coyly. "The story is you met someone on the road."

"It's not like that," he said. "She was just a friend, someone I was helping." He smiled a little behind his cup, sipped some of the coffee, and almost spit it back in the cup. It tasted like oil.

They looked at each other until he could not stand it and lowered his eyes to his coffee. "You've changed your hair a little," he said.

"Ok . . . my hair. You didn't ask me to come down here for a review of my hair," she said softly, but urging him now to get to it.

He brought out a paper lunch sack, wrinkled and creased from use, stained from a long-since-eaten Pastrami sandwich. He laid it on the table between them.

"Happy Valentine's Day," he said, smiling, his face folding painfully with effort.

"What is this?" she asked.

"Open it." He pushed it closer.

She unrolled the end of the sack and looked inside. She squinted then looked up at him, then back in the bag. "What is this?" she asked again, tentatively.

"It's my heart."

She looked at him again, and then back at the bag. She reached in and gently brought it out. It was a velvet pouch, sewn and shaped as she expected, deep red, filled with something, maybe sawdust. It felt strangely warm in her hands. There was a gold safety pin attached to it.

"It was a gift, but I earned it, believe me," he said. "I got it while I was . . . out of town."

He tried smiling again, his face awkward and stiff. "It was quite a trip. I would love to tell you about it sometime."

She laughed a little. "Some guys come home with tattoos . . ."

He didn't know what to say next, and he could feel panic welling up in him. Before she left him, the last thing she had told him was that he didn't understand real intimacy, didn't open up enough. He was distant; not cold, but not engaged. She didn't say he was heartless, but they both knew what she meant. He had a chance to defend himself, but he didn't. He had just looked down at his hands and willed his love to be felt. And then she said goodbye and he was lost.

"I can't take this," she said, rolling the paper bag closed. She flipped her hair back from her face. "This isn't what you think. This doesn't make us 'in love;' it's just a metaphor, a symbol. You need to feel it," she touched her own chest, leaning toward him, "here. And so do I."

Her words cut through him like a carbon-tipped blade. He blinked quickly, startled by his own tears.

"I know, I understand, but listen to me now," he said, trying to bend the words to his will. "I sense that you do feel it, and I feel it too, but it is in every part of me, every molecule burns with the feeling, I just haven't had a way of telling you. When you said goodbye to me, I left here to find what I needed, and I would have done anything, gone anywhere, to bring it to you. I know how I feel about you, about us, I have it in me, in spite of how I appear." He waved his hands up and down his torso, the hinges and pulleys ratcheting his point.

"I know it is more than just having a heart," his voice cracking now, "but now that I have one, I know it means nothing unless I can give it to you."

Her hands slid between the cups and touched his fingertips lightly and he looked up to see what her eyes would tell him. But she was already moving up, away from the table. He watched her go through the diner's door, stop for a fraction of a second that was nearly a lifetime, look back at him, and then the bells clanged goodbye behind her.

He waited. His hands sought each other on the tabletop and held on, treasuring the memory of her touch. He watched the door and waited. He would wait forever.

The waitress hovered for a moment, swirling coffee in a glass pot in one hand. "Is she coming back?" she asked. And she looked at him, finally, and saw the tears running down his face.

"Oh, Hon, you need to take care of that," she said, pulling some napkins from her pocket, "or you're going to be a mess in the morning."

He turned his head to look at her, his neck creaking, and offered a small laugh. "Oh, I won't rust."

Just then, the tin bells came to life as the door opened, and they both looked up. He held his breath and felt his heart pounding in every part of him.

Hope this finds you a friend to the sparrows, and the boys who shoots the arrows,

David

WOODEN VALENTINE

February 2016

Greetings from *il sogno si avvera,*

Cobwebs tinged with dust stretched across piles of scrap wood, pieces of art abandoned and then adopted by the spiders. The workshop was a calamity, filled with projects in various stages of completion; some dangling from the ceiling, others piled in corners, some clamped in place where the woodcarver left off working on them.

There were three-legged stools and ladderback chairs, elaborately etched boxes, a deacon's bench, picture frames, toy wagons, bowls, and spindles. Creations destined for life elsewhere, waiting in the purgatory between the idea of them and reality.

He stood at his workbench, the lanterns flickering at either side of him, bathing the woodcarver in gold. Behind him stretched two oval shadows, converging in a grayish heart shape laid out behind him on the floor, stippled in sawdust.

243

He worked there day after day, month after month, shaping and forming wood into creations sometimes only he would understand at first. Years poured over him and fell like wood shavings at his feet.

His face was still. His eyes had stopped seeing what was in front of him, and now he was lost somewhere else, seeing another time. His hands were resting on the piece he had been sanding, forgotten now on the crowded bench.

His hands were cracked and calloused, the nails rimmed with the vestiges of dark stain. In the decades he had worked with oak and cherry and pine he had aged like wood, darkened in marbled colors from where time had left its patina.

Outside, darkness had already absorbed the world around his windows. He had lost track of the time and worn away another day, sanded it off moment by moment until night was all that was left.

His eyes flickered and he came back to the room. His lips parted beneath the scruffy white mustache and he took a breath. He turned his head slightly and glanced up at the old clock that pecked at the silence.

There was not a day he didn't think of her, but on this fourteenth day in February, the same day he first lost her, she was branded in every pulse in his chest. Each time he breathed in he smelled her, every shadow held her possibility, each sound might have been her saying his name.

He slid his hands from the piece he had been sanding, looking down at its lifeless form where it seemed to mock him, the shape not quite what he hoped. His face changed for a moment as he looked closer at his work. The arms and legs were good, but he needed to spend time on them to make it perfect. Perhaps tomorrow.

He turned from the bench and shuffled across the room and then settled on the worn cushions of the settee. She would be here soon.

He wiped his hands on the apron, both caked with the fine white powder from the sanding cloth, the effort merely trading the dust back and forth. The room was cold; he had not tended to the fire and now he felt it in his bones. He sighed and waited.

In one moment, he was alone with only the sound of his breathing and the steady tempo of the clock. And then she was there.

She sat next to him, lovely, graceful. Her hair, the color of newly cut cedar, was swept up in that magical way she kept it, wild but contained for now, like so much of who she was. She was wearing a yellow dress, his favorite. He did not look directly at her for fear she would not be there. He watched her smile from the corner of his eyes.

She rested her hand on his and his breath caught, and he pressed his lips closed to stifle a sob.

"I am so grateful you are here, but it has been a long year. I miss you," he said. "I am not as strong as I was when you first left, and the time is harder to pass alone."

"I know," she said. "I feel that. But you know I am with you, don't you Joseph?"

He smiled at this, felt the laugh in him. She would call him Joseph to tease him when he was too serious. Or Little Joe. It was something she brought from America.

He finally felt the courage to look at her and he felt the warmth spread over him.

They sat and talked, trading whispers back and forth, laughing now, then quiet again. He told her about the year that had passed, the things he had made, and the people who came to the workshop. The conversation drifted to their shared memories and he felt lighter just being in those moments again with her. The night swept by them marked by the metronome on the wall; he didn't dare look to see how many hours they spent talking. And then he paused and took a breath.

"I love you more than I knew. And now that I know, I am too poor in words to tell you," he said, now unable to look at her for a moment. He sniffed and the tears that had slipped along the creases under his eyes touched the edge of his glasses. He raised his other hand to swipe the moisture on his cheek.

"Love brings us such delight, doesn't it?" she said, taking both of his hands in hers. "But it is not just a gift; it comes with a price. You shouldn't be sad at that cost; it is part of what binds us to each other, the joy of being together, such as this, and the ache that we feel when we are apart. It is each part of the same thing."

He looked at her again, his mind working, trying to find how to say what he felt, knowing that the morning would be coming and their time would end. He spoke her name and she smiled at him, and he felt something in him fill a little more.

"My Joseph," she said. "I must be going soon, but I am not going to leave you alone." She tilted her head and held him with her eyes, the color of deep, rich mahogany. He started to say, "I don't understand," but her look told him he would know what she meant, and he trusted this with his very soul.

Now he did not want to look away from her, not ever. In his mind, he saw them sitting there from that moment on, wherever that took them. The thought gave him peace, and his eyes closed for a moment. And when he looked again, she was gone.

He sat looking at his hands where her hands had been, the dust swept from his skin where she held him. He sensed the room getting lighter as the morning seeped into the room.

There was a soft rustle from his workbench. He looked up, saw the morning light now overpowering the lanterns hung over the bench. The sound again, more distinct, the gentle tocking sound of wood against wood. Something was moving there.

He straightened on the settee, poised to stand but afraid to move.

He stared at the workbench and saw the movement now. There was a gentle cough, and a plume of sawdust rose above where he had been working.

His mind whirled, not knowing what he was seeing, still feeling her presence and hearing her words, trying to put it together with the impossible transformation on his workbench.

And then his son sat up.

Hope this finds you wishing on a star,

David

COWPOKE CHRISTMAS

December 2020

Greetings from the telling,

The sun had already dipped beyond the foothills, and the land left behind lost the color it wore that morning and soon turned gray. In the low places, the dark already took hold. Hoke nosed his horse through the sage until he found a clear spot he liked, tugged the reins, and Paco stopped. They had been riding for most of the day, not in any hurry, but they were both tired.

He swung down from the saddle, grunting a little as he stepped into the hardpack. He patted Paco's rump and then led him near the stand of pinyon pine trees and tied him off. He pulled the saddle, dragged it a ways, and flopped it into the dust.

"Here we are, home again," he said, loud enough to cause Paco to look up. Hoke went about gathering wood for his fire and then rolled a chunk of a deadfall a few feet to give himself something to sit on. He crouched over the litter of dried wood and struck a match, held it to the shavings he put under the kindling. The knuckles of his hands were scarred and swollen, a history of ropes and fights and hammers and horses and steer. One finger was missing on his left hand, a crude ending to a disagreement in Nogales.

The fire came to life. There was a moment of smoke but then the flame surrounded its prey, devouring it slowly. The orange and yellow fingers caressed the wood, changed the twigs to light. The yellow flickering glow showed Hoke's face, creased with years of life out on the range.

"How are you, my old friend?" Hoke asked the fire. Sap hissed and popped on one of the logs. Hoke turned to his rig and pulled out a pan and his coffee pot, dug around and found coffee and hardtack and, in the bottom of his stained saddlebag, some jerky. He filled the pot and set it on rocks at the edge of the fire and waited for his coffee to boil and chewed on his leathery repast.

He spoke into the flames: "Yusser, this is about as good as a man could want. Purty night like this, nothing but the world around me; I can't imagine a better life. Well, no sense in it otherwise, being this is where I am." He and the fire nodded in agreement.

Above him, the constellations formed ribbons of light against the velvet roof. A few stars launched themselves into streaks of life, off to places none below could imagine. Hoke looked up, smiling at the show. "I'm the mayor of Twinkle Town," he said to the fire, laughing, cocking his head at the sky. "Sovereign over all I survey." The fire chuckled with him.

The night cloaked the world. Hoke soaked in the silence and the isolation, kept company by his tin cup filled with coffee and the soft whispers of the fire. He chewed his meal, washed it down with the coffee, and then stopped.

Hoke looked at his hands, tried to sum up when was the last time he knew a date, and then came to a firm conclusion, rooted in mostly instinct. "Sumbitch, it's Christmas eve. Or purt'near." He slapped his knee and laughed. The fire sparked at him. The two of them delighted in the discovery.

"We should celebrate," he said to his friend, and reached into the leather bag, pulled out a metal flask. He unscrewed the top and ran his sleeve over it, tipped it back, and felt the hot taste coat his throat, warm his innards. He breathed in the night air, felt the heat of the corn whiskey. "Now," he said to the fire, "this is a thing we should mark. Only the finest cognac fer us." He spilled a little on the fire and watched his friend lick it in.

Somewhere in his saddlebag was a Bible, or what was left of it. He couldn't read any of it but liked the feel of it, so kept it with him. And glad of it, because on a few nights he needed to tear a page out to start a fire. He always took off his hat when he did, outta respect and all. He knew some of the stories in the Good Book; his Ma had told him enough times. Tonight, it seemed like he should say some words about it. "Listen here," speaking to the flames, "I got a story to tell." He took a deep breath and told it.

"So, this same night, long before us, or railroads, or telegraphs," he said to the fire, "there's these fellas, a-keepin' watch over their herd. And, uh, angels come on 'em and scairt the tar out of 'em." Hoke stopped to laugh, then: "And these fellas evidently weren't armed." He laughed again and slapped his own Colt on his hip. "Lest them angels mighta ended up holier than thou."

"Anyway, these fellas, I tell you, were just drag riders like us'n." The fire seemed unsure, but flickered interest, and so Hoke continued. "Yessir, there they was, watching their herd, biding their time, and the angels come up, and they were shore afraid. And the glory of the Almighty shone around 'em, just like this here." Hoke waved at the whirling constellations above him. He took another pull on the whiskey. The fire leaned in, quivering in anticipation.

"They said, these here angels, said to these cowpokes, 'Fear not, we bring y'all good tidings. Tonight, a Savior is born. And there's gonna be peace on earth, and good wills for men,' is what they said. And then them angels all flew off like a flock and went on up to heaven."

Beyond the ring of light the fire made, the earth was dark and quiet. The rocks and the trees and the sagebrush waited, wondering where the story would go. Hoke took another pull and pushed his hat back a bit. "And these boys, they was a whooping and hollering, on account of what the angels tole. They set out to town to see the baby Jesus."

"And they come a ridin' into town at a gallop and found that Jesus was born right out in the shed behind the saloon. 'Magine that. Savior an' all, right there in the shed, 'longside donkeys an' what have you. Not putting on airs. And these cowpokes was just flat-footed, and they took off their hats," Hoke pulled back his own tattered Stetson, "and they paid respects."

The fire flared brighter, swept up in the story, the flames leaping up into the cool night air. Hoke pressed his hat back in place and took another tug at the whiskey. He leaned in toward the fire.

"And these boys went out and told the world what they seen. Yusser, they was the first messengers, like Pony Express riders for the Lord. These regular cow punchers, not a silver dollar between 'em, and them angels picked 'em to tell the world these here good tidings."

"See, these boys knew that this Savior was for them too, not just the Bible thumpers. They was all sorts of bad, some outlaws, truth be told. But they saw this little baby Jesus, come right in where they live, and tell them they was all right. And peace on earth. Mebbe there wouldn't be no wars, or no more settlin' hostiles, and maybe people would just be neighborly."

251

"And wouldn't be no straw boss talkin' poormouth to you, and no townfolks telling you to move along. And if a fella found a piece a land he liked, mebbe some would let him put up a cabin, have a garden an' all. And wouldn't no one come tell him he had to go sleep in the sagebrush."

"Wellsir, that's what them fellas told. They went around saying what they saw, and you know, people liked hearin' it, and them what told it felt fine saying it."

The fire shone, smiling at its friend, lit the joy on his face for the night to see. Hoke smiled broadly and leaned in once more.

"And me and you, we's just like them fellas that told the good news. Just saddle bums, mebbe, on our last plug of tobacco, mebbe, but we was worth telling this great thing first. And we was plenty good to tell the rest of the world, too. And that right there's a dang good thing to say about a fella. Makes a fella proud to be what he is."

Hoke leaned back and took a sip, offered the last to the fire and capped the flask. He looked up from the flames and saw the cloud of witnesses form above him, galaxies of light and life. He took off his hat, and paid respects.

Hope this finds you sharing the news,

David

Hope this finds you living

"We are a part of a mystery we do not understand, and we are grateful."

~ Brian Doyle

RUNNING TOWARD THE LIGHT

September 2005

Greetings from before the dawn,

I am running in the dark. The only sound is my shoes striking the pavement, my breathing, and the swish of my reflector vest against my shirt. Directly behind me is a full moon, adding a silver light in between the trees that hang over the road. Otherwise, it is dark. Dark-dark.

I am plodding along, not yet fully warmed up. In the dark, I cannot judge my speed, a disorienting feeling that I try to ignore. I am not really paying attention anyway, because I am thinking about something else. I'm thinking about a different darkness.

This Friday marks two years since my Dad died. It was a morning just like this one, straddling two seasons, when I stood at a hospital window and watched the sun come up and trade fall temperatures for summer. It was just like this morning, except it seemed like it would stay dark forever. Up ahead I see a line of mailboxes that suddenly moves from the side of the road and bolts across the pavement. A group of deer, or perhaps ostriches for all I can tell in the dark, making a last-minute decision to cross in front of the lone runner.

I remember waiting in the hospital hallway, feeling the day coming on, pressing my head against the glass of the window, and urging the sun to brighten. In the pale light outside the window, a half dozen stories from the ground, a ladybug fluttered by.

I am trotting in the dim grayness, occasionally made paler by the streetlights. As I move through my little town, I hear an alarm clock going off through an open window. Somewhere in the dark, a lawn sprinkler spurts and sputters as if it is angry about being awakened this early to irrigate pointlessly into the misty, dew-soaked lawn.

I don't think of my Dad every day, but often enough that I am aware of him being gone. I don't dwell on the time surrounding his death, but every once in a while something reminds me. Like a morning like this.

I circle through town and make my way out into the farmland. I am heading back west now, and I see the moon is setting in a violet-blue horizon. A haze along the trees matches the fog in the low places. All is periwinkle for just a short while before the sun crests the other horizon behind me.

I think of the time when my Dad passed away as a healing time for my family, since he was ill for a long time. But that did not spare us any of the grieving. That was the dark part, the part you don't want anyone to go through. With all the support, having family and friends to lean on, faith to draw on, and memories to hold on to, it can still be a hard, dark time.

The road splits the cornfields. The morning has brightened

enough that I can make out rows of birds on the power lines. I hadn't noticed the sun vaulting over the tree line behind me, but I can feel its warmth on my back. The farmland flattens out and now I can see more than two miles down the road.

We celebrated my Dad's life, made toasts to his health, shared the stories with other people who came to console us. We laughed and cried and vowed to make a positive experience of it all, all the while knowing that there would be a darkness we would have to outlast.

I run past farmhouses, tractors gleaming with dew parked in the driveways. One house has a life-size wooden statue of a grizzly bear on the front porch. I am really glad I didn't run into it in the dark a little while ago.

The months have flown by; all manner of life has taken place since my Dad died. Less and less talk about heartache, more and more the days filled up with all the things we do while we are living. Maybe that is why, somehow, I didn't realize I had come out of the dark grief. There was no defining moment, no sudden relief.

Ahead of me is my shadow, stretched forty feet down the centerline, dodging in front of my footsteps. I run faster; the shadow does too. I am old enough to know better than to try to overpower it, so I close my eyes and breathe in the fresh smells. I open my eyes and take in the beauty of the morning.

This week a family from our church entered into this darkness of grief, when a wife and mother, too young to consider such things, passed away. It seems like I should know what to say at this time, give some comfort, tell them that the dark time will pass, but I am at a loss.

A rooster crows, the rural counterpoint to the alarm clock I heard a few miles back in town. There is a dog running in the cornfield next to me, a small dog by the sound of its bark. I don't know what it is chasing, but if enthusiasm counts for anything, he'll catch it.

I offered my condolences, took in their brave faces, with the everything-will-be-all-right smiles. But their eyes held grief, eyes that looked into the time ahead without the woman they loved and saw darkness. I can't tell them that the darkness will fade and that the pain will lessen. They will see it on their own, with time, through faith and prayer, and with the help of friends and the hand of God. But they will not know it from me telling them, even if now were the time.

I have been out here for just over two hours, and I feel like I have been running for two years. I have picked up the pace now, my body finally working as well as it can, given my age. I cut south for a mile to run toward home, and the sun is peeking through six-foot high cornstalks beside me.

Now I turn east again, turn toward the sun. The darkness has faded into the west. My shadow is still with me, that remnant of darkness, but it is behind me now. I can choose to look back at it, or I can look toward the light.

I run toward the sun, toward the light.

Hope this finds you with your shadows behind you,

David

JACK AND LILY

March 2022

Greetings from the witness,

Jack opened the front door and welcomed me in. He wore a suit and tie, which is all I've ever seen him wear. His clothes were from a generation before but were good quality, and well pressed. He was a slight man, made more so by the eight decades, but the suit gave him some size and a formal dignity.

We stepped into a generous foyer, and he said the proper things that a gracious host says, and called out "Lily, our guest is here." He walked ahead of me a few steps, and then turned and took the arm of a small, plump woman, coming down the hall. "This is my bride, Lily."

There was something remarkable about this moment, a tiny glimpse into a marriage of more decades than I had been alive. The two of them, both smiling, not only at me but in delight at being together.

Lily gushed and welcomed me to their home, her words lightly accented from another language, long left behind. She wore a dress, a fashion bookend to her husband. Her hair was parted sharply, dark brown with a henna tone, held in place by a small pin.

She invited me to the kitchen where she had been cooking and had me sit at a small table. She served us all coffee, strong and dark in delicate porcelain cups. She offered me a plate of the dessert she had been making, something sweet and chewy, honey and dates and almonds.

In whatever time dissolved around that table, we sat sipping coffee and becoming friends. We talked about family, about our community, Jack seasoning the conversation with well-used clips of wisdom for his younger admirer. The kitchen was cozy, and even as we sat there in our Sunday Best, I felt relaxed and welcomed.

Lily shooed us out of the kitchen while she tidied up, and Jack took me to the lower level, showed me his office, "Where I make my calls . . . and so on." It was a man's warren, with a desk and the usual bit of clutter. The walls were lined with awards and plaques and commendations, photos of him shaking hands with dignitaries. We talked of his passions, his faith, and a little of his history, which was a much more complicated tapestry than could be covered in one afternoon.

We left his den and soon I was a little lost, making our way through the halls. The house, which from the street was imposing, was larger than I thought. We went back to the kitchen, where I thought I might say my goodbyes. Jack stood next to his wife for a moment, his hand gently on her shoulder. She turned to me.

"Would you like to see the house?" Lily asked. She was smiling, radiating the message. "Of course," I said. "I would love to."

We wound through the foyer again, made our way up the stairs and through hallways, past bedrooms and the "servant's stairway."

"Of course, we never had servants," Jack was quick to say. I was dutifully impressed with the décor and the furniture, the rugs and art. Lily was proud of their home, a small indulgence for the two of them, whose lives were themes of humility and service.

We arrived back on the main floor and walked through a spacious living room lined with ornate furniture, a formal room, with brocade, lace, and patterned pillows. They showed me things they had collected or been given and said the names of the people in the paintings and photographs. We admired the things together, and the two of them shared pieces of their history.

After the conversation seemed to settle, I stepped back toward the foyer, and took a breath to thank them for their hospitality. I turned to face them, and Lily stepped up, holding her hands out.

She looked up at me, a little flushed, slightly breathless. "Would you like to see the house?" she asked.

I hesitated just a moment and turned to Jack. There, in the eyes of one of the kindest people I've met, was a deeper tenderness, one born of a lifetime of love and devotion. His face did not change, and he made no sign that his wife had said anything remarkable.

"Of course," I said to Lily, "I would love to." I glanced at Jack for just a moment, and saw a faint smile, and nothing else.

We followed Lily back through their home, as she guided us through the story of their family. This piece of furniture, this painting, a gift from a friend, a memento from a wonderful trip. Here is the hallway with pictures of family, the elegant rugs, the neat bedrooms, the servant's stairway.

In time we were standing in the living room again, admiring the elaborate furniture, the art, the keepsakes. I complimented Lily on her taste and her rich hospitality. She smiled and blushed beneath her heavy makeup. Jack walked me to the foyer and shook my hand, looked me in the eyes and thanked me. A moment later, Lily was there with a plate of the sweet dessert to take with me.

I turned to wave at them, framed in the front door, two people who allowed me a glimpse of the life they shared. Behind them stretched myriad halls of experience, which showed in the way they held each other beneath the limestone and brick arch.

Many knew Jack and Lily better than I did. This vignette, thirty years ago, sees them after nearly sixty years of marriage, lives of challenge and victory and heartbreak and love, and love, and love. They are both gone on to another place now, and the world spins on, changes, grows, and groans without them. But not without the mark they made here.

The love they shared, what I saw in that tiny slice of time, was stronger than the frailties of living, stronger than the limits of a lifetime. I know, in my own heart, they loved each other forever, and forever and for whatever comes after.

Hope this finds you believing,

David

WAITERS

July 2005

Greetings from out in the fringe,

Any place I have ever visited, I have gotten up early to run. There is a different taste and smell, a different feel in the early morning, and I am always curious about what a place is like during that time. I enjoy the freshness and promise of the new day; it would be all that I write about if I could come up with a way of not repeating myself.

I have seen incredible beauty. I have been inspired by sunrises, awed by creation, in nearly every place I have traveled. I've watched the sun come up over Edinburgh, Dallas, Atlanta, San Diego, Sydney, Chicago, Wounded Knee, Baltimore, New York, St. Thomas, New Orleans, and countless other places. On beaches, in parking lots, in giant cities, in small towns on nameless roads, I have gasped for air while I run, and had my breath taken away by God beginning the day just for me.

And I've seen something else, almost without fail. I see the people who are waiting.

In the dim light of the predawn hours, I see them drifting together in small huddles, talking in low voices, or just waiting. They are the people waiting for work.

The migrant workers and day laborers. They are clustered around light posts or under trees on corners where they know a man will come by with a truck looking for a few guys to do something. They squat at the curb or sit on rocks or lean against trees, waiting. Waiting. Waiting.

I run by people waiting for buses that will take them to their jobs. Women in maid's uniforms, men in coveralls, standing beneath the bus stop sign, where the grass has been beaten back to bare earth from the many people who waited there.

I always say hello because it seems polite, but in the dark they are not always comfortable answering. Sometimes they watch me go by, maybe they will wave. Some just stare ahead or look away to avoid contact with me. Others seem not to notice me.

There are others I see when I run. They are waiting for something, but it's impossible to know what it is without knowing their story.

I see men sleeping in doorways, surrounded by their belongings, wearing their net worth in order to keep warm. Cardboard, newspaper, scraps of clothing are pulled around them to give them shelter while they sleep. I see others waiting next to shopping carts, or under awnings, or sitting on exhaust grates to keep warm. Some are toothless, dirty, unshaven, wrapped in rags. Others seem remarkably well-kept, considering they live on the street.

I run by these people in the cracks and crevices of our society; offer a hello or exchange a nod with those who look up as I pass. We do not fear each other. They know I have nothing to offer them, and I want nothing from them. I think we have curiosity in common. They must wonder what compels a normal person to get up at this ungodly hour and run. I wonder what they are waiting for.

Some are there by choice, some are not. They are someone's parents who couldn't handle the stress, or someone's daughter who became an addict, or an alcoholic. Some are victims, true casualties of racism or mental illness or violence. They have had bad breaks, or made bad choices, or been handed a bad deal. And now they wait.

They wait for someone to give them spare change, or to offer them a meal, or to give them a ride or a place to stay. They wait for a guy who owes them money to come back, for their lotto number to hit, or for life to get better. Some wait to be saved.

I can run by and run on with my life. I am working on my cardio; I am not the guy to save people. My nature is not to pity those who wait. I want to pull them up and tell them to quit waiting, to do something. But I don't think that is what they are waiting for.

You will never see most of the people who wait. They will be in shelters or at the food bank or in jail or in the unemployment line. Some will be working a lousy job, waiting for something better.

By the time the sun is up, these people who wait will evaporate. They will have made their way into their day, to work or to panhandle or to sleep in shade or out of the snow. They will have been prodded along by policemen or shop owners or by the jackals that prey on those who wait.

I feel compassion for the people I run past in the waking hours. I will probably not save anyone, but I can do what I can do, same as you. I can be kind. I can give money without being cynical. I can offer my time to help where it matters. I can offer encouragement. I can point out the sunrise. I can tell you about the people who wait.

Hope this finds you with your hand out,

David

DISTANCE

March 2020

Greetings from right here,

There is a physics paradox someone once shared with me, and it goes like this; if you are one foot from a wall and you move half the distance to the wall, and half the distance again, and again, and again, you are now 3/4 of an inch from the wall. From then on, in theory, you can continue to move half the distance at a time and never reach the wall, because the distance, even at the molecular level, always remains.

Distance, like time, is a construct we developed to measure our reality. One can say that there is nothing flexible about either; they are facts, they are measured scientifically. They are truths.

Except in human interpretation, which is the only reason these constructs exist. This is where we have to season our truth with magic. In a few minutes, you may wonder what these words mean or what value they have, and I will ask you here to be patient.

Hope This Finds You

The passage of time as we see it, not as the clock measures it, varies enormously depending on our perspective, which is our reality. An afternoon with a loved one seems to go on forever, is filled with amazement and joy. Time is suspended. An hour in the hospital waiting room seems like days, and an hour with a friend over coffee is barely noticed. Time, this immutable truth, set in place before we existed, held on stage by the planet's inexorable expansion, is blurred and twisted by our response. Now think about distance.

For children, distance is a concept so abstract they must apply imagination. Their experience, and so their interpretation, creates the need for magic. Ask a three-year-old how he got to gramma's house, whether by car or plane, and he will have to invent the answer. If we look at things with that imagination, we get a feel for what still happens to us, if we allow it.

Distance has mystified me, even as an adult. I have stood at the edge of the Little Mojave and looked across a hundred miles, with no idea what the distance meant. I have stood on top of the Rocky Mountains and marveled at the curve of the earth, not knowing what it was I was really seeing because it is so incomprehensible.

It is the same when I look at the stars, which science can explain but the experience of which demands imagination, whimsy, even magic. Some stars, at such great distance that their light is making its way to us maybe thousands of years after they blinked dark, appear in our lives like fairies.

Someone can explain distance, whether meters or light years, and I understand the concepts. But in my life, where the distance intersects, it is almost always perception. It is my reality laid over the immutable truth, and that creates my truth.

On the morning I turned 19, I woke in a hammock at the base of Mt. Harney, nested near the edge of a small lake, on the west end of

South Dakota. It was damp, the snow still melting, the cold holding me hostage in the shadow of the mountain. I waited for the sun to breach the trees and pushed lower in my sleeping bag, greeting my birthday.

The distance from where I sit to that place is measurable; I can look at a map and figure it out, give a number to it. But the way I see it, the way I am living it, it is RIGHT here. Just now when I thought of going there, I saw myself there already. I know how to get from point A to B but that is like explaining a dream right now. There is no sense of distance except "I am there." My perception of the distance blurred long enough to feel the time compress, the miles shimmer, the cars and planes and shuttles and walking and running all scatter, and I am there.

I can do this magic because of the intense emotional and spiritual connection to the place. It does not alter the world; it alters me. The sense of time and distance is turned into this mosaic, this blur of the truths we know scientifically. In its place is how I perceive it all. If no one bothered me with ticks and tocks and klicks and blocks, that would be how I would see the space between here and there.

The physics paradox about the distance to the wall is just a way of demonstrating a truth. It does not take into consideration that I can feel the wall, sense its shape, texture, coolness. It does not allow that my perception of the distance is all that matters. I know the wall, I know the plaster, the wooden frame behind it, the nail, the thickness of the paint. I even know the energy it took to construct it. Even though the science, the fact, says I am never going to actually bridge the distance before me.

Here's why you want to think about this. The word "distance" probably has never been spoken so often as it has now, usually in a disruptive way. Somehow in the days to come, you will have distance pushed into your life. It will separate you from the people and experiences you've relied on for the joys in your life. My friends, the distance is only as great as you allow it to be.

I think this magical perception of distance and time is one we purposely dull. Like a lot of things, we no longer experience the passage of these truths the way we did when we were three or four. For good and practical reasons, I suppose, but there will come a time when those are not as important as the magic. Perhaps the time has come.

If you are apart from the places you wish for, you can go there. If the people you want to be with are separated by distance, then find a way to dissolve it; it's in your power, and in a way, they make it possible. Don't be intimidated by the magic. It was given to us by the same Creator of distance and time.

Hope this finds you piercing the truth,

David

David Scott Smith

LIFE WISH

February 2022

Greetings from the peak,

Yesterday I went for a run in the winter, a twenty-mile loop in our arctic mitten. I left home in the dark; the sky was scoured clean by pitiless winds, and only a few stars braved the blackness. The world outside my balaclava was covered with snow, held in place by brittle cold.

The first miles gave me no reason to be optimistic, which I knew better than to pay attention to. Knowing better doesn't always matter.

By the time it was light, I was in the farmlands, where the wind sliced over the open places and erased any register on Fahrenheit. It reshaped the snow, sending sensual shapes over the icy roads. The condensation on my mask froze solid and my legs went numb from the relentless cold.

I stumbled across the snow, slipping on the ice underneath, moving so slowly it might not record as running. I'll admit, if I hadn't been ten miles from my front door, I would have given in to the temptation of a warm fire and a steaming cup of coffee. I was tired, the week's miles stacking up in my legs, now two leaden trunks under me.

I was fumbling with my water, frozen slush in the bottle, when the sun finally crested the horizon. In that moment, the light painted the white canvas with a brilliant gold. The sun found a range of tiny peaks in the snow thrown off the road, a tiny replica of giant mountain cousins around the world. When I just focused on them, I could have been watching the sunrise on the Himalayas; the stark white, the blue shadow, all burnished in the warm light that seemed to only exist on the peaks. Then I remembered something.

A few years ago, I watched a documentary about a group of alpinists, mountain climbers, a small cadre of world-caliber adventurers who decided to summit Meru in India. It's not the highest mountain to climb, or the most famous, but it has been nearly impossible to accomplish. The story is compelling on its own, but the foundation of it tells something else.

Conrad Anker led this team, a world-renowned climber who has summited Everest three times. He has climbed some of the most challenging peaks in the world, and for every ascent, there are at least as many failures, some of which nearly cost him his life. Most of Anker's friends have died by falling off mountains, which led someone to wonder if they all have a death wish.

"It is not a death wish; it is a life wish," he said.

I wrote it down when I heard it, and seeing it later by itself on the page, it seems a little dramatic. Except I know the context. The answer was to say: we have found the edge of human endurance, the most demanding challenge to our abilities, we have tapped the essence of our human experience. When we are there, we are fully alive. Since we have been there, we must go back again, not to tempt death, but to call to life.

My adventures never take me to anywhere close to death; at worst, maybe some sore legs and a numb face. I don't live that life, not this time around. Occasionally, though, I realize how any of us, even plodding runners, can scrape away the dullness. We find ourselves touching what is in us, sometimes undiscovered, and it grabs us by both wrists and demands we pay attention: it is a life wish.

Occasionally, people will hear about my running and shake their heads, wondering what I am running from, if there are some masochistic tendencies at work, or perhaps I am trying to prove something, or some other experience from the template of their own life. But in truth, it's because it's one of the places I find my life wish.

Conrad Anker said, "Meru is the culmination of all I've done and all I've wanted to do." It took three tries, monumental efforts, which nearly killed a good friend. And they went up because that's where life is. And he says this: "The summit is what drives us, but it's the climb that matters."

In ten weeks, I will run Boston. These long runs are building blocks for that challenge, but I need to remember that they are also part of the climb. It's the climb that matters. The climb, the miles, the hours of practicing the violin, or raising a child, or teaching or hacking at words to make them say what you want to be heard. It is the climb; that's where the life wish is.

We have to invest ourselves to find it; we have to reach past the easy, the expected, or the status quo. That's why sometimes it looks dangerous or reckless or crazy, or worse, like a death wish. So, we do it, because from the moment we are created, and every time after when we are shown where it is, we wish for life.

Hope this finds you wishing,

David

HALF DOME

June 2021

Greetings from the fullness,

Each step became a journey of its own.

Last Tuesday I celebrated my birthday, and all our birthdays, by climbing Half Dome, a rigorous ascent from the floor of Yosemite to the granite knot that towers above the tree line. In the twelve hours we spent making our way up, and then down, I became reminded of one of the more important lessons of living.

A week later I can still feel the fullness of the day. Not only in my sore muscles, but in the new places that have been sparked in my mind.

A few years ago, I read a book by Jedidiah Jenkins and watched a small documentary about his travels on a bike from Oregon to South America. The adventure was interesting, but the lesson was what stayed with me.

"Routine is the enemy of time; it makes it fly by. When we are a kid, everything is astonishing, everything is new, and so your brain is awake and turned on," he said. He goes on to say that as you get everything figured out and create a routine for life, the alertness goes away. Soon the moments slip by unnoticed, and then hours and days. Suddenly years pass.

The cure, Jenkins says, is to create a life that demands you pay attention, be startled, afraid even. To learn, to engage, to feel full emotions. In this awakened state, we slow down time by crafting hours of living. Remember those endless afternoons when you were seven years old?

None of this is new. I am only writing this out to remind you, and me, of the importance. I have been thinking about the days my children were born, and those when loved ones passed, and other celebrations and challenges and adventures. They were exhausting and demanding and thrilling and in all of that, those days were filled with such rich experiences they kept me in place. Time stayed with me instead of racing away like a mischievous puppy.

I woke on my birthday and stood in the dark with my brother Douglas and sipped coffee in the light of our headlamps. We whispered our plans back and forth, giggling, already anxious to begin, but waiting for the rest of our group to wake. I wasn't sure what to expect, but I couldn't wait to see it unfold.

I am tempted to share some of the day, but I'll admit I'm intimidated. It was a holy time for me, and in this moment, I feel unprepared and unworthy to describe it all. And still, I am going to damn well write it anyway, because that's why I am here.

There were moments like these: climbing the ragged steps along the Mist Trail, the waterfalls raging in the dark next to us, our headlamps weaving in the air around us like manic fireflies.

Unnerved, nearly crawling up Sub Dome, feeling the open cliff pulling at me. Trembling muscles, gasping for air, heart hammering in my ears, whispering, "give me strength . . . run the mile you're in . . . help me to feel you here . . . "

The air grew thin as we rose up into the mountain, and then we could no longer take our breath for granted. Hundreds of strangers wishing me happy birthday along the way or joining in our warbling song to celebrate. And the ultimate mash-up: dangling from the cables of Half Dome as my brother led a group of strangers strung down the mountain behind us in 'Hap-py birth-day, dear Dav-ud," gasping with the effort.

Praying for my sister on the summit, under a clear blue dome that stretched over mountains as far as we could see in any direction. Finding the perfect place, tucked inside the mountain, to keep her stone for the next millennium. The whirl of feathers in my chest when I looked over the edge of the cliff to the valley below. Watching Lee's tangerine escape; bright orange bounding across the white granite, and then disappearing into the air beyond the edge. Then, reluctantly, easing back down the cables, and into the trails below, the sun baking us in the bright places so we would love the cool of the tall pines.

Lunch by the river, sitting on a log eating mangled peanut butter and jelly sandwiches. We were entertained by a single trout idling in the clear, emerald water. I didn't want to leave. "I love this," I said. The others, packs already on their backs. looked at me quizzically. "This," I said, gesturing around us. I meant the idyllic setting, and moments later, I meant all of life.

The trail was rarely predictable. Rocks and roots and uneven places, we wound through the mountains on switchbacks that were not polite about their intentions. I had to pay attention to where I was stepping or I risked tripping and falling, which in some places could be fatal.

My legs were so tired that I had to will them to move, to have a conversation with them, asking them to partner with me again, just another step. Each step became a journey of its own. It is a different experience than simply getting up and perambulating to the mailbox and back, unaware of the miracle your body is performing.

We stumbled into camp a dozen loaded hours from when we left and dropped our things and then, inspired by Cali, made our way back to the Merced River and waded in. I sat in the icy water and felt the muscles go numb; my aches washed away with the dust on me. I felt the weight of the day, a welcome weariness that comes with filling the hours with new experiences, with learning, astonishment, fear, exhilaration, wonder, and the deeply rooted passion that still brings tears to my eyes.

We are given the chance to feel life this way in ordinary moments. Preparing a meal, fixing a flat tire, planting flowers, making coffee. It comes to us in perfect sunrises, ping pong conversations, interruptions, long hard laughter, overwhelming love. It comes because we allow it, choose it. When we fill our moments with intention, deliberately choosing awe instead of emptiness, we become companions with time. It falls into step with us, keeps pace as we move through our life. In time, there are the infinitesimal and the infinite, and what separates the two is what we fill the moments with.

Hope this finds you taking your time,

David

LESLIE

August 2021

Greetings from a brother,

"Who would want to live a life where you didn't love someone so much that you didn't grieve their loss?" ~ Tom Skaff.

The world spins, and it spins among other planets, and they all spin in orbits and the galaxies spin in sensual whorls, and the universe curves in wider swaths into whatever is beyond. And in all of that, my sister Leslie slowly moved to the edge of the inexorable motion and held for an eternal moment, and then she let go. And the momentum of her life sent her into some new place.

On Thursday, Leslie quietly let out her last breath, and with it, became something new. She has not ended, she has changed. And we, complicated and simple things left behind, changed with her.

It takes unique courage to know what will end your life. Most of us will never face that knowledge. We will only be vaguely aware, perhaps, that one day we will walk through a door to something else. Maybe it will be some sudden thing no one could anticipate, or any combination of human experiences that may lead to a slow slide to a quiet end.

My sister knew with certainty what would cause her last breath, and she watched it unfold in front of her. She approached that uncompromising promise with grace and dignity and a beauty that held even to the last day. Even writing these words, now blurred in the prism of tears, I am in awe of her strength.

Some months ago, I was talking with Leslie on the phone and, for reasons I didn't know, I read to her from a book I love entitled *One Long River of Song*. Brian Doyle wrote of a nun he met once who said, "No one beats cancer, cancer is a dance partner you don't want and don't like, but you have to dance, and either you die, or the cancer fades back into the darkness at the other end of the ballroom."

Even as I shared the words, I felt terrible, as if I were telling her some other bad news she didn't already know. But she did. Cancer is rarely beaten; it is to be endured. It has no purpose other than to destroy, and yet humans, my sister prime among those, turn that purpose into something filled with hope and patience and perhaps the best of what we are created for.

Not many weeks ago, I sat in the shade of bamboo trees and held my sister's hands and we talked and listened, and in that spinning together of us, and of her soul's mate, Bill, we suspended time. We set aside the incessant change, the incorruptible procession of us, and just learned what humans always want to know. That we matter, that we are loved, that we will be remembered. That if life goes on without us, it's not without us.

We invited God to join us, and He was present but remained quiet and didn't take questions. I think we were given the space to ask and answer and wonder and be afraid and seek possible, and that's what He wants us to ache for.

Someday if you ask me, I will tell you about that afternoon, an impossible stretch of time, given Leslie's condition. I have a rich life, and a history of experience that is filled with variety and adventure and remarkable moments. But, my friend, that piece of living we had in those few hours, is matched by rare few companions.

Among the things we talked about were the mysteries of life, including the ultimate mystery; what happens when the struggle ends and we greet the cloud of witnesses, when we take whatever steps we are given to reach forever and after. There are so many beliefs, so many philosophies, so many stories about what to expect, each as meaningful as the next, as meaningful as the Avett Brothers' lyrics:

"Will I join with the ocean blue? Or run into a savior true? And shake hands laughing . And walk through the night, straight to the light, Holding the love I've known in my life, And no hard feelings."

My faith tells me that what waits for us beyond the door of our life is more wondrous than Leslie or I could imagine. That makes me smile, because she knows now, and because my sister wouldn't need "wondrous." She only wants to see those she loves who wait there. She hopes for a place where she can sit with God in the warm shade of bamboo and feel the ease of a conversation with someone who loves her. She only wants to see our lives here unfold, and that we are all right even as we miss her.

There is no escaping grief, and still, I want to ease the pain for those who can't bear it. Someone told me a long time ago, I wish I could say who it was, that when someone leaves us, they also create ways to stay with us: "Look for signs of them." Meaning, small ways to know they are there, watching our lives, part of us in a new way.

There, in the smile of her sister, there in the love of her husband, there in the mannerisms her children took from her. Perhaps in the clacking of bamboo in the wind, or the sigh of wind chimes. Perhaps in the sunflowers that stood for her brave dance with an unwanted partner.

I am told that we have in our bloodstreams the dust from stars which last shone a bazillion years ago. That matter never ends, it only changes, and by extension, changes us. We would not be exactly what we are had these supernovas not shone so brilliantly.

This truth fits perfectly with Leslie's life. In the sliver of time she was here, she changed everyone with her light. Each of us, her husband, her children, her brothers and sisters, and her nearly infinite choir of friends, now share Leslie in our bloodstream. It is such a privilege to carry her with us, to show her our lives in the days given to us here. It is a joy to feel her in this way that cannot ever, ever end. And if we want to look for signs of her, we need only look for the glimmer in the eyes of those who love her, that vast galaxy of other stars shining with her brilliance.

Hope this finds you looking for Leslie,

David

JOY AND ACHE

December 2020

Greetings from the diptych,

In nature the two things are wound in one. Every morning begins with these tandem possibilities; the brooding clouds, the dark rim of the world, transformed by the unseen sun, turned to rose and pink sculpture. Each tree groans and cracks even as it grows upward to fulfill its destiny. The sluicing rain, cold and petulant, has in it a beautiful sound, makes new sounds in creeks, staccato amidst leaves. The same water that floods and destroys gives life, reflects life.

Summer begins, and in that first moment is the end of summer, already created, already laced in its birth. I celebrate Summer even knowing that with each warm breath I exhale, the season is diminished. They are not separate things; they are parts of the same thing.

In the most important parts of my life, I have felt these two things joined and inseparable, for so long that I cannot unknow them in this way. Joy and ache, each wound at their roots to one another. Our lives grow this way, and they weave together with others with both elements as one.

My mother spoke her last words just two years ago, and there is a pleasure in having heard them, and in the same experience, grief. I own the experience of her with us; alive, raising a family, pushing us into the world, watching her live her own life, being a part of ours, so many reasons to smile. And joined with that, the sorrow of her last days, and now her absence. Her memory is a joy, and the loss of her is an ache.

I love to write, it is a passion, and within that are struggles. When I write, I choose words that I hope express what I am feeling, that I hope will make the ideas understood, and will matter to someone reading. In the choosing there are words not chosen, maybe better, maybe other. I won't say it's anguish, but the process has both joy and ache. The words on the page calling to those left in the pen, friends, soon to be neighbors, urging their partners out. There are times I stare at the ideas waiting, and wait with them, hoping somehow for the muse to intervene.

But ultimately, I am a writer, not a waiter, and so a word in the hand is worth two in the bush. There is a little pain, and a little regret, bound to a great deal of satisfaction. There are also times, a sweet confluence of muse and moment, when the words simply fall onto the page, and I am only here to shepherd them gently until I can set them free to you. I feel like a bystander who watches as God creates a rainbow, and then I sign it. It is hard, and it is beautiful.

This sense of having both the pleasure and pain in one thing may sound conflicting, but it doesn't feel that way to me. Instead, it feels like a natural reminder to appreciate the complex wonder of any moment I am given.

Some time ago I spoke with someone who was struggling with

her work, and she decided the only way to go forward was to harden herself, to not care so much. In the kindest way I could, I asked her not to put up a shell against the world. I didn't know her well enough to say any of this, but something in the moment would not be resisted.

"We don't need people who care less," I said. "We need people who are the opposite of apathetic. Yes, it means we are going to feel pain because of it, but that's where the living is. You have a boyfriend; you are in love with him, right?"

"Yes."

"And even knowing that he is not perfect, he will forget, he will be inconsiderate, he will make mistakes, and that will cause you pain, you don't want to give up the chance to love him. Right?"

"Yes," she said, now probably wondering why she ever said a word to me.

"Because you already know the ache and the joy are wound together, that one makes the other richer, more possible, more authentic. If you hardened yourself to that, you would miss the beauty of being in love. It is the same in every ordinary exchange with the people we meet."

Crossing the finish line of the marathon is an experience with myriad sources, but nothing demonstrates the ache and joy more literally for me. I run for the pleasure of running, but my role as a good animal is to seek "arete," to find whatever excellence I am capable of. Running the marathon plumbs that depth. Thousands of miles of pressing the body toward being better means pain, suffering, even. And the marathon provides a stage to prove the effort. The victory of completing the distance is never, ever, separate from the agony of the miles.

Raising children is a living example of joy and ache. Even as they cry their first breath, we celebrate what it means. Their first words, first steps, broken hearts, each struggle we share with them, we know these form the foundation for a rich life. We also see time slip over them, and even as we love who they become, we sometimes long for the intimacy of who they were.

This strange time of separation has been hard for most of us, and I felt it this week. I long to see my friend, and I don't know when life will allow it. In the missing of him I am aware of our history, our friendship, and a hint of our future. This ache, this dull feeling of his absence, is the binding of the joy. It says, "Here is someone you care for, who has given you countless reasons to laugh and think and even cry with gratitude. He has this place in your life, and even missing him is a privilege of knowing him."

Time presents to us as now, and as the past, and as the eternity in front of us. In each moment there is the potential for joy and ache and both. We experience this moment and lose it, enjoy the memory and miss the moment, look toward a future and ache to be in it. The seconds and hours and years whirl by and inside all of them are these two parts of us braided as one. I am just reminding us that the intensity and power of our life, and what we love in it, is made more so when it is refracted through the tiny prism of the time we are given.

The ache reminds us we are alive, that we have experienced, and it is joined with the joy, the laughter and love and hope, the moments we cherish, and expect again. We needn't always give in to one or expect the other. The contrast of these partners makes sorrow bearable, and maybe inspires us to value the beauty more.

Hope this finds you with each and both,

David

GENEROSITY

July 2020

Greetings from beyond the iron bars,

I have been talking with friends around the country who are now struggling with the resurgence of the virus, watching their communities become restricted again. It is a discouraging thing to have life become nearly normal again, only to have that autonomy we sometimes took for granted wrested away.

It is not the only challenge we have, not even addressing the impact of the illnesses and death that comes with it. But after months of dealing with these limitations, the frustrations are apparent.

When I was a boy, one of my favorite books was *The Count of Monte Cristo*, by Alexander Dumas. In this story, the main character, Edmond Dantes, is falsely imprisoned for life, and after years in jail, his spirit is nearly broken. Then, he makes friends with another inmate who provides him with a gift of education, teaches him mathematics, the beauty of literature, the history of the world, as it was known in the 1800s.

I haven't thought about the book in years, not sure if it is still in my library. It is a complex book, but what brought it to mind was the catalyst for Dantes' salvation. Faced spending the rest of his life in tortuous confinement, he found hope in friendship, and in learning how large the world really was through his education.

Even as we set aside concerts and races and family reunions and travel, even as we chafe under the masks and lines and inconveniences, we are given hope, if we allow ourselves to see it.

Many of you have made positive changes in the face of the disappointments. You have adapted and found creative ways to keep fun in your life, to maintain relationships, to fill the hours with something beyond even the screens that seem to dominate our lives now. You are a part of my inspiration for this morning.

Another book, now one of my favorites, is *A Gentleman in Moscow*, by Amor Towles. In order to tempt you to add it to your collection, I will tell you it is a rich, beautiful story, written in a style that is a delight to read. And this; the main character, Count Alexander Rostov, is sentenced to life imprisonment in the Metropol Hotel in Moscow.

There are many wonderful lessons of humanity in the story, but this morning I have been focused on Rostov's philosophy of life, probably dormant until called upon in his confinement. The first lesson he calls on is: "Master your circumstances, or they will master you." Sometimes an ambitious thought, but consider it. It does not demand you change your circumstances, but merely be the one directing them.

The next, a more lasting ideal that he holds to for a generation, he explains in a conversation with a new friend. In this sentence, he shows what we are all capable of. It is the thought of a mature, seasoned person, who understands that life will not always offer exactly what we expect.

"As both a student of history and a man devoted to living in the present, I admit I do not spend a lot of time imagining how things might otherwise have been. But I do like to think there is a difference between being resigned to a situation and reconciled to it."

Each of us is given this morning to respond to. We may not always be given the freedom of all choices, but we have the first one, how we take this moment and do with it as best we can. It isn't failure to accommodate around a difficult passage in life. It is how we make the best of each moment. Go to a dictionary and read the definition of "reconcile," and I promise you will find the word "harmony."

The two Counts found freedom in their confinement. They passed through frustration and disappointment and hopelessness, and reached moments where the spirit, the "arete" given them by their Creator, provided an independence from their prison, one that could not be taken back.

I know what waits in my day today, it will be challenging. Before I turn to face the first thing, I will gather strength from the gifts I am given, a wonderful collection of experiences and memories, the company of my family and friends, and the fullness of love in my life. Yes, I am building gratitude in my life to balance what could take its place.

In a scene from *A Gentleman in Moscow*, Rostov responds to a friend who points out his rich life before his arrest. He says, "Life has been generous to me in its variety." This obscure sentence in a four-hundred-page book gave me a tool that I treasure. I ask myself, and now you, "How has life been generous to you?" The answer is also the answer to how we can summon the gratitude, and the courage, to combat what life may offer instead of what we expect.

I didn't even have to ask myself this morning, the answer was given to me as I sipped my coffee. There is magic in the

Summerlight. It eased out of my day yesterday in a brilliant orange, dotted with the tiny beads of fireflies seasoning the grass. This morning, it began with a pale blue tint in the gray, pushing the last of night into shadows in the woods, and then this whiter light, the first hint of what the sun will be today. Two fawns stood in the grass as the sun buttered the green around them. Life has been generous to me in its beauty.

Let's go change our world.

Hope this finds you feeling free,

David

RIBBONS

June 2021

Greetings from the first blush,

I have been smiling at glimpses of Summer through the windows each morning. Lingering in the low grass, in the first light, in the one crystalline jewel of dew. Driving around town with the windows down, I felt her there, delighting in my choice of music. Seeing the cameo hue in the clouds at dawn, and by eternal magic, again at night.

The warmth came on the feathers of tiny robins on their first flight, in the mourning dove's soft hymn. The spaces in the trees closed in with green. Miniature fawns teetered on matchstick legs between new leaves and shoots in the yard. These were more than hints.

A few days ago, I pushed into the Flint River in my kayak and paddled without much ambition downstream, winding several miles outside of my little town. It has been a long time, but the rhythm came back quickly.

I paced with dragonflies cruising along the water's surface, feeling like they were happy to see me, sometimes hitching a ride on my boat. The water was clear so I could see the rocks and billowing seaweed.

I was vaguely aware of the date on the calendar, somehow connected to the sun and stars, and how it would announce the arrival of my favorite season. But I could feel it in me already. My morning coffee, the first sips usually in dark, were in the pale false dawn. The daylight eased back the twilight, painted yellow ribbons on the green even before the world was ready to be awake.

On the river, I soon lost track of moments and just felt the flow of the water around me. The blue arced over the trees, dotted with small birds, and now a heron, graceful and also outlandish, as if shuttling back to some prehistoric era.

Along the shore, a dozen impossibly tiny ducklings skittered in the water, mostly hidden by the foliage there. I was still delighted by them when suddenly there was a flurry of air and feathers and their mother crashed through the grass and into the water, squawking and splashing, wildly swimming at me.

She was angry, her wings up as she skittered across the water at me, protecting her little brood. I was so taken aback that I wasn't sure how to respond, so I paddled quickly away. She chased me for far longer than I expected, close enough for me to see the wild look in her eyes. Even this morning I am smiling at the courage, and how well her strategy worked.

I coasted on the indifferent current until I scraped onto some rocks and held there, rested my paddle, and let everything relax for a moment. I could feel the ebb of the river, felt it align with my pulse. I let my mind drift back over the week. There have been these little moments of warmth and light, filling the gray places left by winter, and even the damp spring. I felt Summer close around me, the dampness on my skin, which is already darker from the sun. My reverie was shaken as a fish leapt from the water in front of me, just out of the water, to take an innocent victim from the swarm of gnats floating there.

There were flowers growing in the woods near me whose names I don't need to know. Snowmelt from months ago fills the streams and lakes and wanders down ways made by God before we all existed and pools in small places, reflecting the sky and trees. In an invisible magic dance, it finds its way into the sky again and rains into the green and makes it greener. It makes rivulets and creeks and ponds, and it makes this river.

I floated by people fishing, some serious, others merely using their lines to make ripples in the water. Two men stood in a flat boat fly fishing, a graceful ballet of arcing lines, living bookends over the water. I paddled quietly past another pair intently casting from shore, and yet another walking their boat along the shallows.

The river led me past small islands, kids splashing on the bank, a single deer timidly watching me from the shallows. A choir of geese paddled to a steep edge and somehow, in perfect choreography, walked into the woods for some appointment none of us will know.

Hours passed unnoticed and I glided to a stop in a small opening in the thick growth along the shore. Landing where I once set a leaf free, where we sent my mother's ashes into this same river. The kayak made the water giggle around its hull and then eased onto the shore and set me back onto the other earth.

Yesterday I set off into the farmland to carve a twelve-mile rectangle in the humidity, and I came home smiling as I walked to the end of my driveway. I felt like I had been given a gift. The morning stood bright and warm, a gift to me to celebrate Father's Day, and the arrival of Summer, my friend, maybe my closest companion.

In the time I moved along the roads, wearing mostly sweat, I pushed past the opening I was given and into Summer, into the season of ripe fruit and rich sunsets, of fireflies and thunderstorms. I thought about moving down that river, which felt like gliding on my bike, or hiking in the woods, or this very run, all linked to being immersed in nature, in Summer.

This morning, watching the first light reflected in the rain pooled outside my window, I know I have been invited to another beautiful season of life. I can't wait.

Hope this finds you living it up,

David

Acknowledgements

I want to express my deepest gratitude to …

My friends and family for encouraging me to create this book, and to my wife Suzanne for supporting me, giving me the space to chase this long-held dream.

Katherine Smith and Jennifer Smith for helping me with creative decisions, for reading my work, and cheering me on.

Carson, Harrison, and Sawyer for giving me so much raw material to write about all these years.

Jewell July, my editor, for bring her professional polish to my work.

My friend and mentor Eileen Button for shining the light on the path. For coaching and editing and gently pushing me into the best choices.

And to every one of you who took a kind moment to tell me that the words mattered, I am so very thankful.

Hope this finds you feeling loved,

David

About the Author

David Scott Smith is the author of Monday Moanin', a weekly essay written without fail every Monday since 1999. He was a humor columnist for the *Flint Journal* and has written for *Runner's World*. He is also the recipient of the prestigious Red Quill Award, conferred to a rare few in Mrs. Ahearn's Fifth Grade class. He is a dedicated storyteller at the Moth and will not resist the urge anywhere else. He spends his free time in Michigan running, exploring, watching the sun rise, and searching for the perfect cup of coffee.

Sign up for more

If you would like to read the weekly essay Monday Moanin', you can sign up for notifications, or have them emailed to you. Also, receive news from the author about new books, events and other announcements.

www.davidscottsmith.net.